W9-BMM-220

JUMBLE®

Mania

A Collection for Passionate Puzzlers

Henri Arnold, Bob Lee, and Mike Argirion

TRIUMPH
BOOKS
CHICAGO

Copyright © 2004 Tribune Media Services, Inc. All rights reserved.
Jumble® is a registered trademark of Tribune Media Services, Inc.

This book is available in quantity at special discounts
for your group or organization.

For further information, contact:

Triumph Books
601 South LaSalle Street
Suite 500
Chicago, Illinois 60605
(312) 939-3330
FAX (312) 663-3557

Printed in the United States of America

ISBN 1-57243-697-2

CONTENTS

JUMBLE®

Mania

Classic Puzzles

Unscramble these four Jumbles, one letter to
each square, to form four ordinary words.

LEEBI

MOBIL

YEASUN

YURSLE

I was working on a story

I've had it with you!

WHAT THE BUSY
REPORTER GOT
FROM HIS
GIRLFRIEND.

Now arrange the circled letters to form
the surprise answer, as suggested by the
above cartoon.

Print answer here: A " ☐☐☐ " ☐☐☐☐

Unscramble these four Jumbles, one letter to
each square, to form four ordinary words.

GILTH

BEPOR

DUNCIE

MOABEA

SOME PEOPLE WHO
DON'T PAY TAXES
IN DUE TIME—

Now arrange the circled letters to form
the surprise answer, as suggested by the
above cartoon.

Print answer here:

JUMBLE®

Unscramble these four Jumbles, one letter to
each square, to form four ordinary words.

LOVEN

REGUP

YALMIN

TECJOB

WHAT THE GUARD
CALLED THE KEY
TO THE JAIL, AS HE
THREW IT AWAY.

Now arrange the circled letters to form
the surprise answer, as suggested by the
above cartoon.

Print answer here: THE ⬡⬡⬡ ⬡⬡⬡⬡⬡⬡

JUMBLE®

Unscramble these four Jumbles, one letter to each square, to form four ordinary words.

AMFER

SIVOR

UNCOOP

GERUDD

HE COULDN'T THINK STRAIGHT BECAUSE HE ALWAYS HAD THIS.

Now arrange the circled letters to form the surprise answer, as suggested by the above cartoon.

Print answer here:

⬡⬡⬡⬡⬡⬡ ON HIS ⬡⬡⬡⬡

Unscramble these four Jumbles, one letter to each square, to form four ordinary words.

ACEEP

YATHS

HISRAP

CUSPER

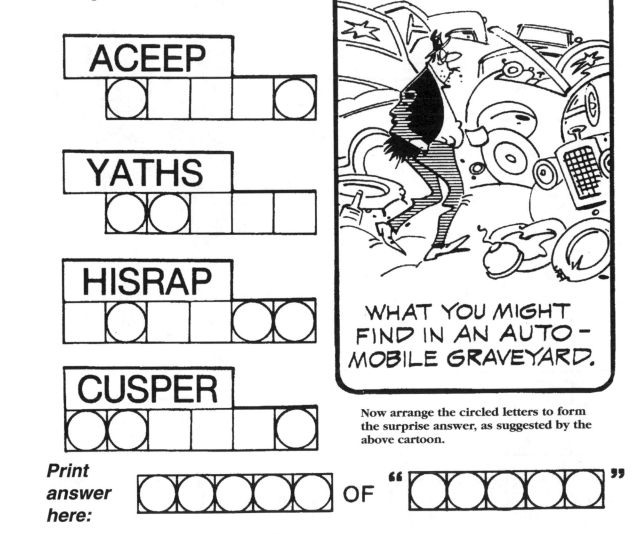

WHAT YOU MIGHT FIND IN AN AUTO-MOBILE GRAVEYARD.

Now arrange the circled letters to form the surprise answer, as suggested by the above cartoon.

Print answer here:

☐☐☐☐☐ OF " ☐☐☐☐☐ "

JUMBLE®

Unscramble these four Jumbles, one letter to
each square, to form four ordinary words.

HOTOT

GUBOS

TICUND

CYRIKT

Just in case

THEY DRANK TO
EACH OTHER'S HEALTH
SO OFTEN THAT
THIS HAPPENED.

Now arrange the circled letters to form
the surprise answer, as suggested by the
above cartoon.

**Print answer
here:**

JUMBLE®

Unscramble these four Jumbles, one letter to each square, to form four ordinary words.

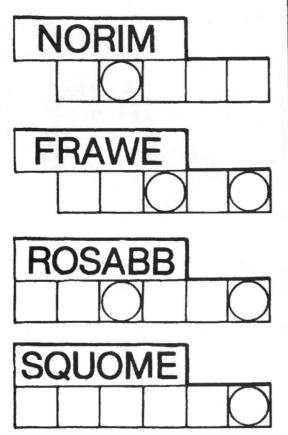

NORIM

FRAWE

ROSABB

SQUOME

WHAT BRIEFS ARE USUALLY "WOVEN" FROM.

Now arrange the circled letters to form the surprise answer, as suggested by the above cartoon.

Print answer here:

JUMBLE ®

Unscramble these four Jumbles, one letter to
each square, to form four ordinary words.

STURY
◯◯◯

THANC
◯◯◯

FORTYS
◯◯◯

SHIVAL
◯◯

What! No food for
such a long trip?

I'm
hungry!

WHAT IT TURNED OUT
TO BE WHEN THEY
FORGOT TO HOOK ON
THE DINING CAR.

Now arrange the circled letters to form
the surprise answer, as suggested by the
above cartoon.

Print
answer
here:

A " ◯◯◯◯ " ◯◯◯◯◯

JUMBLE®

Unscramble these four Jumbles, one letter to
each square, to form four ordinary words.

SOEBE

DYRYL

CROLIF

NIDIOE

WHAT THE BLUSHING
BRIDE WAS TURNING,
WHICHEVER WAY
ONE LOOKED.

Now arrange the circled letters to form
the surprise answer, as suggested by the
above cartoon.

Print answer here:

JUMBLE®

Unscramble these four Jumbles, one letter to each square, to form four ordinary words.

LEVVA

AMMAD

CHEWEN

DRIFOL

We're all in the same boat these days

PAY LOANS HERE

EVERYBODY WAS IN DEBT BUT IT'S PERMITTED.

Now arrange the circled letters to form the surprise answer, as suggested by the above cartoon.

Print answer here: " ☐☐☐ – ☐☐☐☐ "

Unscramble these four Jumbles, one letter to
each square, to form four ordinary words.

DRYBE

LORGY

DELNAH

FIGNAC

SOUNDS LIKE
A FISHERMAN'S
DANCE.

Now arrange the circled letters to form
the surprise answer, as suggested by the
above cartoon.

Print answer here:

Unscramble these four Jumbles, one letter to each square, to form four ordinary words.

CAMIG

GUVEA

TRAFYC

SAUNAE

How's he gonna get out of THIS one?

WHAT A PERSON WHO LOSES HIS HEAD WOULD HAVE DIFFICULTY DOING.

Now arrange the circled letters to form the surprise answer, as suggested by the above cartoon.

Print answer here:

Unscramble these four Jumbles, one letter to each square, to form four ordinary words.

INCCY

VENAH

SPOCER

EMBURP

WAYS THAT GO STRAIGHT TO THE HEART.

Now arrange the circled letters to form the surprise answer, as suggested by the above cartoon.

Print answer here:

Unscramble these four Jumbles, one letter to
each square, to form four ordinary words.

DORBO

MYLOD

PLECOM

CIVONE

— How dare you! —

THE SNOB WAS
INSULTED WHEN THE
DOCTOR TOLD HIM
HE WAS MERELY SUF-
FERING FROM THIS.

Now arrange the circled letters to form
the surprise answer, as suggested by the
above cartoon.

Print
answer   A   "⬭⬭⬭⬭⬭⬭⬭" ⬭⬭⬭⬭
here:

JUMBLE®

Unscramble these four Jumbles, one letter to each square, to form four ordinary words.

UNOMT

JETEC

TASTLE

HATTOR

HOSPITAL

MIGHT BE THREE THAT COULD PUT YOU OUT.

Now arrange the circled letters to form the surprise answer, as suggested by the above cartoon.

Print answer here: " ⬡⬡⬡⬡⬡ "

JUMBLE®

Unscramble these four Jumbles, one letter to each square, to form four ordinary words.

TIDIO

HECEK

PRETOY

DILVER

But I didn't do nothin'!

HOW HE PROTESTED WHEN THEY PUT HIM IN THE COOLER.

Now arrange the circled letters to form the surprise answer, as suggested by the above cartoon.

Print answer here:

JUMBLE®

Unscramble these four Jumbles, one letter to
each square, to form four ordinary words.

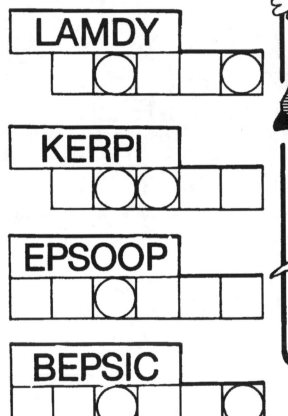

LAMDY

KERPI

EPSOOP

BEPSIC

It's him again! Won't be in.
CLAIMS he's not feeling well

IT MIGHT BE
"ILL-GOTTEN."

Now arrange the circled letters to form
the surprise answer, as suggested by the
above cartoon.

Print answer here:

Unscramble these four Jumbles, one letter to
each square, to form four ordinary words.

TRIVE

PRIVE

NIVIET

HUNCAL

We always assure a good
reception here

THE WARDEN GUAR-
ANTEED THE ENTER-
TAINERS THAT THE
AUDIENCE WOULD
BE THIS.

Now arrange the circled letters to form
the surprise answer, as suggested by the
above cartoon.

Print answer here: A " ◯◯◯◯◯◯◯ " ONE

Unscramble these four Jumbles, one letter to each square, to form four ordinary words.

RYMEC

NYPOH

NIRBON

CIPTED

The traffic was murder today

HOW THE EXECU-
TIONER WOULD HAVE
PREFERRED GETTING
TO WORK.

Now arrange the circled letters to form the surprise answer, as suggested by the above cartoon.

Print answer here:

20

Unscramble these four Jumbles, one letter to each square, to form four ordinary words.

HACOP

GOMOR

GROINI

RUMAID

But he pulls in plenty

WHAT SOME COMEDIANS MAKE.

Now arrange the circled letters to form the surprise answer, as suggested by the above cartoon.

Print answer here:

⬡⬡⬡⬡⬡ OUT OF ⬡⬡⬡⬡

21

Unscramble these four Jumbles, one letter to
each square, to form four ordinary words.

CIEPE

YERAW

CHELEK

SATECK

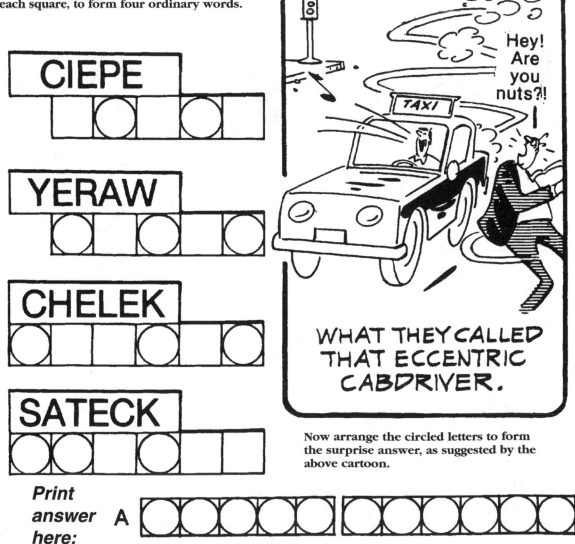

Hey!
Are
you
nuts?!

TAXI

WHAT THEY CALLED
THAT ECCENTRIC
CABDRIVER.

Now arrange the circled letters to form
the surprise answer, as suggested by the
above cartoon.

Print
answer
here:

A ◯◯◯◯◯◯ ◯◯◯◯◯◯◯

JUMBLE®

Unscramble these four Jumbles, one letter to each square, to form four ordinary words.

WATHE

RADIC

ROMMEY

FLAUWL

Goody—blubber!

WHAT THOSE
ESKIMOS LOVED
TO DO AT
DINNERTIME.

Now arrange the circled letters to form the surprise answer, as suggested by the above cartoon.

Print answer here: ⟨◯◯◯◯◯⟩ THE ⟨◯◯◯⟩

JUMBLE.

Unscramble these four Jumbles, one letter to
each square, to form four ordinary words.

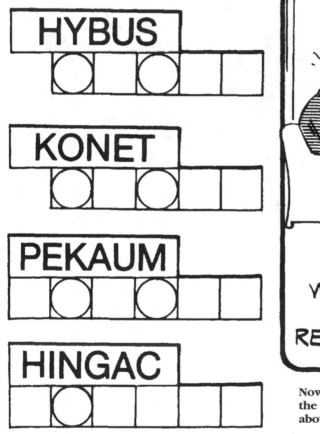

HYBUS

KONET

PEKAUM

HINGAC

WHAT IT WAS FOR
HIM WHEN THEY
REPOSSESSED THE TV.

Now arrange the circled letters to form
the surprise answer, as suggested by the
above cartoon.

Print answer here: A " ☐☐☐ ☐☐☐☐ "

JUMBLE®

Unscramble these four Jumbles, one letter to each square, to form four ordinary words.

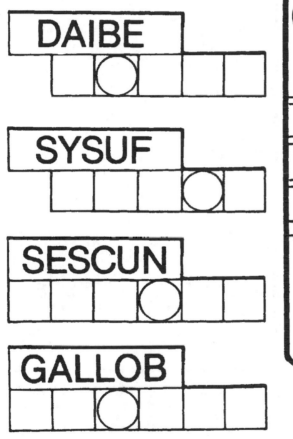

DAIBE

SYSUF

SESCUN

GALLOB

Here's the latest statement

You're not going to like it

PRESIDENT

WHAT THE BOSS WAS "BREAKING INTO."

Now arrange the circled letters to form the surprise answer, as suggested by the above cartoon.

Print answer here: " ⭕⭕⭕⭕ "

JUMBLE®

Unscramble these four Jumbles, one letter to each square, to form four ordinary words.

MYPUB

LAUFT

SILCHE

ALLOCE

Oh, dry up!

HOW THE WAITRESS ACTED WHEN SHE SPILLED THE GRAVY.

Now arrange the circled letters to form the surprise answer, as suggested by the above cartoon.

Print answer here:

26

JUMBLE

Mania

Daily Puzzles

Unscramble these four Jumbles, one letter to each square, to form four ordinary words.

ORNOH

DAULC

UNISCO

ALDLAB

Doesn't recognize his old buddies

WHEN HE BECAME TOP BANANA HE LOST TOUCH WITH THIS.

Now arrange the circled letters to form the surprise answer, as suggested by the above cartoon.

Print answer here: THE ⭕⭕⭕ ⭕⭕⭕⭕⭕⭕

JUMBLE®

Unscramble these four Jumbles, one letter to each square, to form four ordinary words.

CHARN
☐☐☐◯◯

RYPOG
☐☐☐◯◯

ENDALT
☐◯☐◯☐☐

KAJECT
☐◯☐☐☐☐

WHAT SOME NOT-SO-YOUNG ACTORS FIND IT DIFFICULT TO DO.

Now arrange the circled letters to form the surprise answer, as suggested by the above cartoon.

Print answer here: ◯◯◯ THEIR ◯◯◯

JUMBLE®

Unscramble these four Jumbles, one letter to each square, to form four ordinary words.

LUTEL

SQUAH

UIDDEG

DELDUP

WHAT HAPPENED AFTER HE BOUGHT A NEW PAIR OF SUSPENDERS?

Now arrange the circled letters to form the surprise answer, as suggested by the above cartoon.

Print answer here: HE WAS ⬡⬡⬡⬡⬡ ⬡⬡

JUMBLE®

Unscramble these four Jumbles, one letter to
each square, to form four ordinary words.

ENGAM

WESHO

TICUND

DOUXES

FOR NOT SHOVELING
THE SIDEWALK
THERE ——

Now arrange the circled letters to form
the surprise answer, as suggested by the
above cartoon.

Print answer here: ⬡⬡⬡⬡ ⬡⬡⬡⬡⬡⬡

JUMBLE®

Unscramble these four Jumbles, one letter to
each square, to form four ordinary words.

TALPI

NECHE

TIFONY

INMALY

WHAT THEY CALLED
THE GUY WHO
WAS NUTS ABOUT
FISHING.

Now arrange the circled letters to form
the surprise answer, as suggested by the
above cartoon.

Print answer here: A " ☐☐☐☐ – ☐☐☐☐ "

Unscramble these four Jumbles, one letter to each square, to form four ordinary words.

He's going to get elected

And then he'll rob us blind

IN A POLITICIAN, THE GIFT OF GAB IS OFTEN CONNECTED WITH THIS.

NEFIT

INGGA

BALGER

ENGALT

Now arrange the circled letters to form the surprise answer, as suggested by the above cartoon.

Print answer here: THE ⟨⟩⟨⟩⟨⟩⟨⟩⟨⟩ OF ⟨⟩⟨⟩⟨⟩⟨⟩

JUMBLE®

Unscramble these four Jumbles, one letter to
each square, to form four ordinary words.

JARAH

MYKUR

HACCYT

RODIAH

IN THOSE YEARS
STRAW HATS
HAD THIS.

Now arrange the circled letters to form
the surprise answer, as suggested by the
above cartoon.

Print answer here: THEIR " ◯◯◯ " ◯◯◯

JUMBLE

Unscramble these four Jumbles, one letter to
each square, to form four ordinary words.

ROGOF

GIESE

LAWASY

KONVIE

WHEN THEY FILM A
WINTRY SCENE IN HOLLY-
WOOD, THE PROP MAN
HAS TO COME UP WITH
PLENTY OF THESE.

Now arrange the circled letters to form
the surprise answer, as suggested by the
above cartoon.

Print answer here:

35

JUMBLE

Unscramble these four Jumbles, one letter to each square, to form four ordinary words.

REQUE

MOGAD

DEBISE

LETTOU

Listen to what we did today

PEOPLE WITH TIRELESS ENERGY SOON BECOME THIS.

Now arrange the circled letters to form the surprise answer, as suggested by the above cartoon.

Print answer here:

36

Unscramble these four Jumbles, one letter to each square, to form four ordinary words.

KOLEY

GWAON

FABFEL

IMLYRG

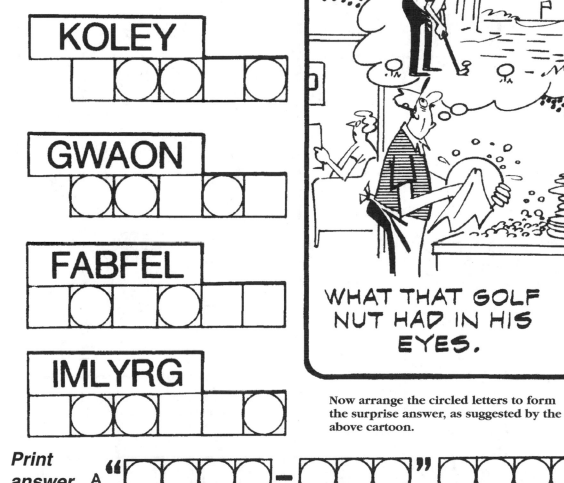

WHAT THAT GOLF NUT HAD IN HIS EYES.

Now arrange the circled letters to form the surprise answer, as suggested by the above cartoon.

Print answer here: A "◯◯◯◯ – ◯◯◯" ◯◯◯◯

JUMBLE®

Unscramble these four Jumbles, one letter to
each square, to form four ordinary words.

TONJI

AVVLE

STUMKE

ABHORR

I'VE FINALLY BOUGHT
YOU A WATCH FOR YOUR
BIRTHDAY, DEAR

Now arrange the circled letters to form
the surprise answer, as suggested by the
above cartoon.

Print
answer "IT'S ⬡⬡⬡⬡⬡ ⬡⬡⬡⬡"
here:

JUMBLE®

Unscramble these four Jumbles, one letter to each square, to form four ordinary words.

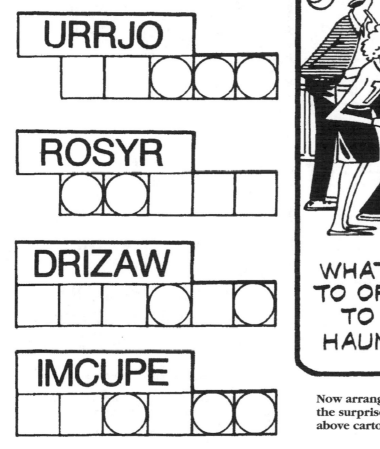

URRJO

ROSYR

DRIZAW

IMCUPE

WHAT THEY HAD TO OPEN IN ORDER TO ENTER THE HAUNTED HOUSE.

Now arrange the circled letters to form the surprise answer, as suggested by the above cartoon.

Print answer here: THE " ⬡⬡⬡⬡⬡⬡ " ⬡⬡⬡⬡

Unscramble these four Jumbles, one letter to each square, to form four ordinary words.

IRRAB

NEVAK

SACCES

HURGOT

WHAT IT WAS
FOR THE PEEPING TOM
WHEN HE WAS CAUGHT
LOOKING THROUGH
AN OPEN WINDOW.

Now arrange the circled letters to form the surprise answer, as suggested by the above cartoon.

Print answer here:

40

JUMBLE®

Unscramble these four Jumbles, one letter to each square, to form four ordinary words.

VEEKO

YAWLB

TELTEK

ENICKS

Sounds like a prowler

MIGHT BE USEFUL IF YOU WANT TO LEARN ABOUT THE "SHOCKING" SECRETS IN THAT CLOSET.

Now arrange the circled letters to form the surprise answer, as suggested by the above cartoon.

Print answer here: A " ⬡⬡⬡⬡⬡⬡⬡⬡⬡ " ⬡⬡⬡

JUMBLE®

Unscramble these four Jumbles, one letter to
each square, to form four ordinary words.

OONES

CEROW

BEWOLB

STEACK

WHAT A NAME
DROPPER IS APT
TO DO.

Now arrange the circled letters to form
the surprise answer, as suggested by the
above cartoon.

**Print
answer
here:** ⬡⬡⬡⬡ HIS " ⬡⬡⬡⬡⬡ "

Unscramble these four Jumbles, one letter to each square, to form four ordinary words.

LOTEX

ALLIV

WEGNIT

HALTEL

I've always believed a man should be the boss

WHAT IT SOMETIMES TAKES TO LAND A SPOUSE.

Now arrange the circled letters to form the surprise answer, as suggested by the above cartoon.

Print answer here: A ⬡⬡⬡⬡⬡⬡ " ⬡⬡⬡⬡ "

JUMBLE®

Unscramble these four Jumbles, one letter to each square, to form four ordinary words.

EEDUL

TYJET

SNUFIO

YUBILS

Makes you want to fall asleep on the spot

WHAT A PILLOW SALESMAN HAS TO BE A MASTER OF.

Now arrange the circled letters to form the surprise answer, as suggested by the above cartoon.

Print answer here: THE ⬡⬡⬡⬡ ⬡⬡⬡⬡

JUMBLE®

Unscramble these four Jumbles, one letter to each square, to form four ordinary words.

KLANB

DUTIA

BEMFUL

SMOTED

WHAT THE INVENTOR OF THE FIRST AUTO-MATIC PACKAGING MACHINE MADE.

Now arrange the circled letters to form the surprise answer, as suggested by the above cartoon.

Print answer here: A ⬡⬡⬡⬡⬡⬡

JUMBLE®

Unscramble these four Jumbles, one letter to each square, to form four ordinary words.

WHART

BASAH

ZURBEZ

ALPECA

WHAT THOSE OLD-TIME RUSSIANS FOUGHT.

Now arrange the circled letters to form the surprise answer, as suggested by the above cartoon.

Print answer here: "⬡⬡⬡⬡" ⬡⬡⬡⬡

Unscramble these four Jumbles, one letter to each square, to form four ordinary words.

TILMI
◯◯◯◯◯

ANBOT
◯◯◯◯◯

PERUSH
◯◯◯◯◯◯

ROTTET
◯◯◯◯◯◯

Gulp!

WHAT THE SUGAR TYCOON GOT AS HE WAS TRYING TO PROPOSE MARRIAGE.

Now arrange the circled letters to form the surprise answer, as suggested by the above cartoon.

Print answer here: A ◯◯◯◯ IN HIS ◯◯◯◯◯◯◯

47

Unscramble these four Jumbles, one letter to
each square, to form four ordinary words.

GOEBT

ROYAF

NEPAHP

PHISAR

FOOTWEA

THE ONLY THING
THAT CHILDREN
WEAR OUT FASTER
THAN SHOES.

Now arrange the circled letters to form
the surprise answer, as suggested by the
above cartoon.

Print answer here:

Unscramble these four Jumbles, one letter to
each square, to form four ordinary words.

SUMEA
☐☐☐☐☐

CEROF
☐☐☐☐☐

SWEDIT
☐☐☐☐☐☐

NIROPS
☐☐☐☐☐☐

Go to Department X-12, fill
that out in triplicate, then . . .

WHAT A BUREAU-
CRAT IS.

Now arrange the circled letters to form
the surprise answer, as suggested by the
above cartoon.

Print
answer A ☐☐☐ ☐☐☐☐ ☐☐☐☐
here:

Unscramble these four Jumbles, one letter to each square, to form four ordinary words.

URIOC

DEFAM

GAMANE

LEPOAR

You've got it all, kid!

SOMETHING A LOT OF WOMEN ARE TAKEN IN BY.

Now arrange the circled letters to form the surprise answer, as suggested by the above cartoon.

Print answer here:

Unscramble these four Jumbles, one letter to each square, to form four ordinary words.

GANET

SOUHE

LYNFOD

EFFOTE

WELL!

HOW THE TRAFFIC COP'S GIRLFRIEND CAUGHT HIM.

Now arrange the circled letters to form the surprise answer, as suggested by the above cartoon.

Print answer here:

51

Unscramble these four Jumbles, one letter to each square, to form four ordinary words.

JEDDA

GNATY

COBORN

NAVIED

THE MEDIA THOUGHT THEY'D BETTER GIVE THE EVENT PLENTY OF THIS.

Now arrange the circled letters to form the surprise answer, as suggested by the above cartoon.

Print answer here: " "

52

Unscramble these four Jumbles, one letter to each square, to form four ordinary words.

PERIT

HISFY

SNIULF

NITIVE

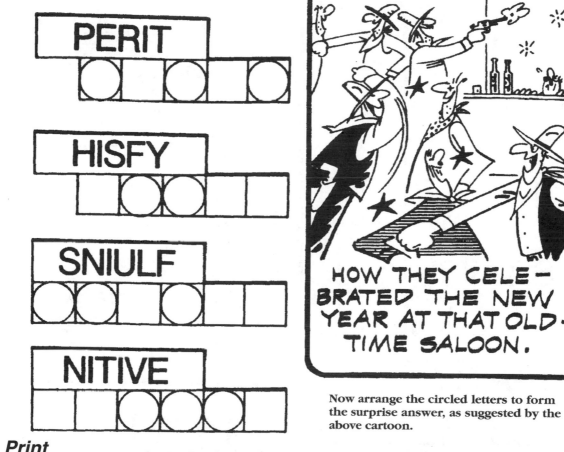

HAPPY NEW YEAR!

HOW THEY CELE-BRATED THE NEW YEAR AT THAT OLD-TIME SALOON.

Now arrange the circled letters to form the surprise answer, as suggested by the above cartoon.

Print answer here: WITH " ⬡⬡⬡⬡ – ⬡⬡⬡⬡⬡⬡⬡ "

PUZZLE 52

JUMBLE.

Unscramble these four Jumbles, one letter to
each square, to form four ordinary words.

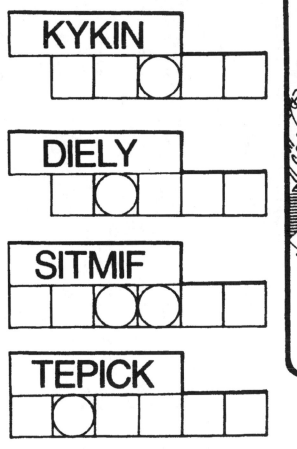

KYKIN

DIELY

SITMIF

TEPICK

WHAT PART OF A
FISH IS LIKE THE
END OF A MOVIE?

Now arrange the circled letters to form
the surprise answer, as suggested by the
above cartoon.

Print answer here: THE "◯◯◯ ◯◯"

54

Unscramble these four Jumbles, one letter to
each square, to form four ordinary words.

STUQE

UPDYM

FINTEC

YOHRFT

WHAT THE KARATE
CHAMP TURNED
RESTAURANT OWNER
SPECIALIZED IN.

Now arrange the circled letters to form
the surprise answer, as suggested by the
above cartoon.

Print answer here:

JUMBLE®

Unscramble these four Jumbles, one letter to
each square, to form four ordinary words.

TIBOR

WEDIP

RAYWEL

VELCOR

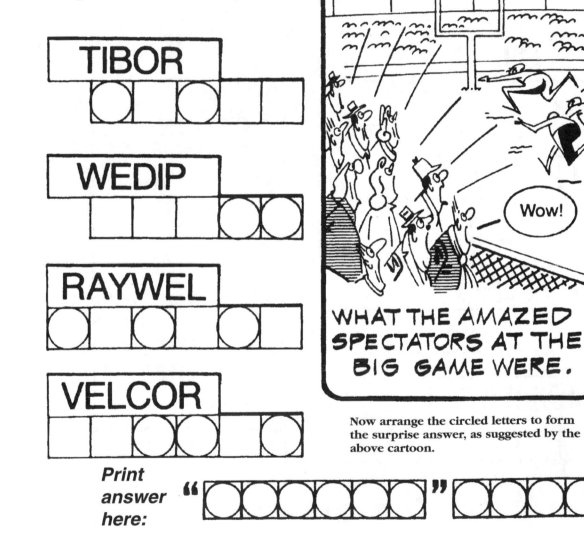

WHAT THE AMAZED
SPECTATORS AT THE
BIG GAME WERE.

Now arrange the circled letters to form
the surprise answer, as suggested by the
above cartoon.

**Print
answer
here:** " ◯◯◯◯◯◯ " ◯◯◯◯

JUMBLE ®

Unscramble these four Jumbles, one letter to each square, to form four ordinary words.

SECAE

CANYF

HALEXE

FIMFUN

Oh, my achin' back

AFTER SHE ASKED HIM TO START WORKING ON THE GARDEN, THE FIRST THING HE DUG UP WAS THIS.

Now arrange the circled letters to form the surprise answer, as suggested by the above cartoon.

Print answer here:

JUMBLE®

Unscramble these four Jumbles, one letter to each squarc, to form four ordinary words.

MIDUH

KNACS

GLANID

WASALY

He has wonderful rhythm

HE LISTENED TO THIS WHILE HE PRACTICED.

Now arrange the circled letters to form the surprise answer, as suggested by the above cartoon.

Print answer here:

JUMBLE®

Unscramble these four Jumbles, one letter to each square, to form four ordinary words.

RAMEF

AWNTY

DIMPER

TASTLE

You look fabulous

I'm almost broke, but I'm thin

THE RESULT OF SPENDING A FORTUNE ON WORKOUTS.

Now arrange the circled letters to form the surprise answer, as suggested by the above cartoon.

Print answer here:

JUMBLE®

Unscramble these four Jumbles, one letter to each square, to form four ordinary words.

TYDIT

ARREM

OURSEA

RECRON

There goes our night out

BILL

WHAT PLUMBING WORK CAN DO TO THE FAMILY BUDGET.

Now arrange the circled letters to form the surprise answer, as suggested by the above cartoon.

Print answer here: ☐☐☐☐☐ A ☐☐☐☐☐

JUMBLE®

Unscramble these four Jumbles, one letter to each square, to form four ordinary words.

HOTOT

GALEL

FIMFUN

LEEMOT

Got a match?

WHAT THE CROWD
EXPERIENCED AT
THE COMEDY CLUB.

Now arrange the circled letters to form the surprise answer, as suggested by the above cartoon.

Print answer here: A "◯◯◯◯◯" ◯◯◯◯◯◯

JUMBLE®

Unscramble these four Jumbles, one letter to
each square, to form four ordinary words.

LOVEC

HASAB

PLUCUF

SPYGUM

FOUND AT
THE SHORE.

Now arrange the circled letters to form
the surprise answer, as suggested by the
above cartoon.

Print answer here: ⬡⬡⬡⬡⬡ AND ⬡⬡⬡⬡⬡

JUMBLE®

Unscramble these four Jumbles, one letter to
each square, to form four ordinary words.

PUBYM

LISEA

INMAYL

SNELET

He doesn't look
very friendly

HARD TO FIND
ON A SHADY
PERSON.

Now arrange the circled letters to form
the surprise answer, as suggested by the
above cartoon.

Print answer here: A ☐☐☐☐☐☐ ☐☐☐☐☐

JUMBLE.

Unscramble these four Jumbles, one letter to each square, to form four ordinary words.

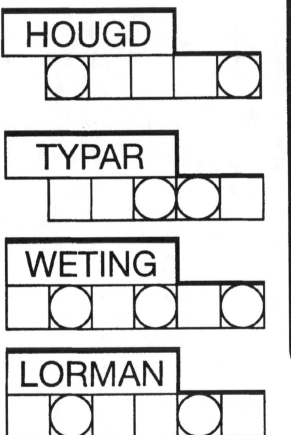

HOUGD

TYPAR

WETING

LORMAN

Make sure the soil is rich in nutrients

THE KIND OF ADVICE YOU GET FROM AN OLD FARMER.

Now arrange the circled letters to form the surprise answer, as suggested by the above cartoon.

Print answer here: ⬡⬡⬡⬡ TO ⬡⬡⬡⬡⬡

JUMBLE.

Unscramble these four Jumbles, one letter to
each square, to form four ordinary words.

DENIK
◯◯◯□◯

USEED
□□◯◯◯

LISHEC
◯◯□◯◯◯

LOFUND
□□◯◯□◯

He doesn't even
know I'm here

WHAT SHE FELT
LIKE WHEN HER
HUSBAND CON-
CENTRATED ON
HIS MUSIC.

Now arrange the circled letters to form
the surprise answer, as suggested by the
above cartoon.

Print
answer
here: ◯◯◯◯◯◯ ◯◯◯◯◯◯

JUMBLE®

Unscramble these four Jumbles, one letter to
each square, to form four ordinary words.

MAUSE

KERCE

FRUGEE

NASTEF

Wait, I've
got more

Sorry, all full

TOUGH FOR A
GARBAGE MAN
TO DO.

Now arrange the circled letters to form
the surprise answer, as suggested by the
above cartoon.

Print
answer
here:

JUMBLE®

Unscramble these four Jumbles, one letter to
each square, to form four ordinary words.

BOAVE

ETHAL

HADEBE

LATHEC

Everything OK?　　We're cool

WHY THE COP
WAS IN THE
JAZZ CLUB.

Now arrange the circled letters to form
the surprise answer, as suggested by the
above cartoon.

Print answer here: HE

Unscramble these four Jumbles, one letter to
each square, to form four ordinary words.

TEAGA

GELBI

HUMILS

NARCLE

...And the monster jumped
out of the bushes...

WHAT THEY
HEARD AROUND
THE FIREPLACE
ON A COLD
NIGHT.

Now arrange the circled letters to form
the surprise answer, as suggested by the
above cartoon.

Print
answer
here: A

Unscramble these four Jumbles, one letter to each square, to form four ordinary words.

BOGUM

VABER

CLUSKE

INMERV

Why won't this #%!!**? thing work?!

A NEW COMPUTER INEVITABLY HAS ONE OF THESE.

Now arrange the circled letters to form the surprise answer, as suggested by the above cartoon.

Print answer here: A ⬡⬡⬡⬡⬡⬡

69

JUMBLE®

Unscramble these four Jumbles, one letter to
each square, to form four ordinary words.

LAIDY

KEDAC

CANVAT

HIGLES

Let's go fishing

AUDITIONS
TODAY

That's a
wrap

SOMETHING
ACTORS LOOK
FORWARD TO.

Now arrange the circled letters to form
the surprise answer, as suggested by the
above cartoon.

Print answer
here: A

JUMBLE®

Unscramble these four Jumbles, one letter to
each square, to form four ordinary words.

CYDEA

TOABB

KORBEN

TIPURY

Have your cards ready, please

Smithers claims he did
all the selling himself

WHAT THE SALES-
MAN DID WHEN
THEY CHARGED
THEIR PURCHASES.

Now arrange the circled letters to form
the surprise answer, as suggested by the
above cartoon.

Print
answer
here: THE "   "

Unscramble these four Jumbles, one letter to each square, to form four ordinary words.

SIPOU

THERB

ENCOUP

CIPEAE

It's beautiful   ...And smells good, too

WHAT A PRETTY FLOWER ARRANGE-MENT CAN BE.

Now arrange the circled letters to form the surprise answer, as suggested by the above cartoon.

Print answer here: A " ◯◯◯◯◯◯ - ◯◯◯◯◯◯◯◯ "

JUMBLE®

Unscramble these four Jumbles, one letter to each square, to form four ordinary words.

HELEC

URUGA

WEREVS

LAFFEB

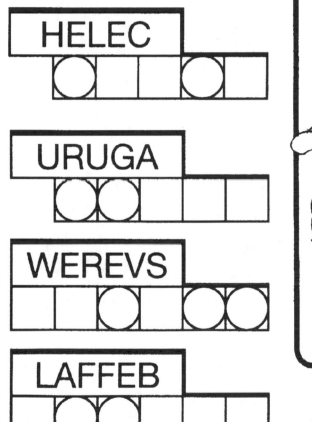

She's gorgeous!

That's why she gets $500 an hour

HOW THE MODEL CALCULATED HER WORTH.

Now arrange the circled letters to form the surprise answer, as suggested by the above cartoon.

Print answer here: AT ☐☐☐☐ ☐☐☐☐☐

Unscramble these four Jumbles, one letter to
each square, to form four ordinary words.

LAROF

CUTOS

UTTOWI

NELKRE

Quitting
time

Not now. It's going good

WHY THE PAPER
HANGER WORKED
LATE.

Now arrange the circled letters to form
the surprise answer, as suggested by the
above cartoon.

Print answer here: HE ⬡⬡⬡ ⬡⬡ A ⬡⬡⬡⬡

JUMBLE®

Unscramble these four Jumbles, one letter to each square, to form four ordinary words.

HIKKA

FIMOT

CODJUN

EKATIN

This is fun

WHAT HE GOT
FROM HIS
KARATE CLASS.

Now arrange the circled letters to form the surprise answer, as suggested by the above cartoon.

Print answer here: A ⬡⬡⬡⬡ ⬡⬡⬡ OF ⬡⬡

Unscramble these four Jumbles, one letter to each square, to form four ordinary words.

PREKO

PROUG

RIELOO

CHELIN

I'm getting exhausted

Stay with it

HOOKING A TWO HUNDRED POUND FISH CAN LEAVE YOU LIKE THIS.

Now arrange the circled letters to form the surprise answer, as suggested by the above cartoon.

Print answer here:

JUMBLE®

Unscramble these four Jumbles, one letter to each square, to form four ordinary words.

YLSYH

OSLOE

CARFIB

YARWIA

She'll be better than ever

She should be, for what that cost

THIS HELPED HIS YACHT SAIL SMOOTHLY.

Now arrange the circled letters to form the surprise answer, as suggested by the above cartoon.

Print answer here: ◯◯◯◯ "◯◯◯◯"

77

Unscramble these four Jumbles, one letter to each square, to form four ordinary words.

DOORE

GUNST

PANDEM

HERVIT

Hot chili, pickles, french fries, potato pancakes...

THE SERVER FOUND THE DINER'S ORDER THIS.

Now arrange the circled letters to form the surprise answer, as suggested by the above cartoon.

Print answer here: ◯◯◯◯ TO ◯◯◯◯◯◯

JUMBLE®

Unscramble these four Jumbles, one letter to each square, to form four ordinary words.

BOTOR

GIBEE

RASTUX

UNSLIM

Late for my meeting, and now this. Why me?

STUCK IN A SNOWDRIFT LEFT HIM—

Now arrange the circled letters to form the surprise answer, as suggested by the above cartoon.

Print answer here:

Unscramble these four Jumbles, one letter to
each square, to form four ordinary words.

CENEF

RAWGE

HOARIM

ALLTOW

Off the starboard,
Captain

Keep her
steady

A GOOD THING
TO DO WHEN
ENCOUNTERING
AN ICEBERG.

Now arrange the circled letters to form
the surprise answer, as suggested by the
above cartoon.

Print answer here: ⬡⬡ ⬡⬡⬡⬡ **THE** ⬡⬡⬡⬡

JUMBLE®

Unscramble these four Jumbles, one letter to each square, to form four ordinary words.

DEPTY

WUNDE

YAHRLD

ORTRER

Whew! Let's open a window

WHAT THE RO-MANTIC SETTING LED TO.

Now arrange the circled letters to form the surprise answer, as suggested by the above cartoon.

Print answer here: A " ☐☐☐☐ " ☐☐☐☐

JUMBLE®

Unscramble these four Jumbles, one letter to each square, to form four ordinary words.

CLOIG

GIERT

NOALOS

SARGYS

Approaching 700 feet

That's enough. We can't afford to waste fuel

ALWAYS A CON—CERN FOR A CAREFUL BALLOONIST.

Now arrange the circled letters to form the surprise answer, as suggested by the above cartoon.

Print answer here:

JUMBLE®

Unscramble these four Jumbles, one letter to each square, to form four ordinary words.

VENAK

UPYTT

TRUGET

SUMMUE

Can I work on the next fitting?

10-14

WHAT A NOVICE TAILOR WANTS TO DO.

Now arrange the circled letters to form the surprise answer, as suggested by the above cartoon.

Print answer here:

JUMBLE®

Unscramble these four Jumbles, one letter to each square, to form four ordinary words.

CELER

CEPEA

RATTAR

LADLAB

Let's have salad tonight

I'll get some fresh bread

A GOOD WAY TO GRAB DIN-NER IN A SUPERMARKET.

Now arrange the circled letters to form the surprise answer, as suggested by the above cartoon.

Print answer here: ◯ ◯◯ "◯◯◯◯"

84

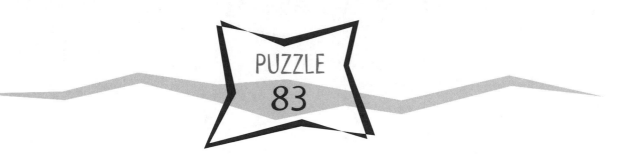

Unscramble these four Jumbles, one letter to
each square, to form four ordinary words.

GIHLT

VELIA

MULEHI

FRILPE

I feel ten years younger

WHAT THE
PLASTIC SUR-
GERY DID.

Now arrange the circled letters to form
the surprise answer, as suggested by the
above cartoon.

Print
answer
here: ⬭⬭⬭⬭ ⬭⬭⬭ A "⬭⬭⬭⬭"

JUMBLE®

Unscramble these four Jumbles, one letter to
each square, to form four ordinary words.

SABIN

RIVOS

MAPCEN

CARNID

Wide right on
two, break

A QUARTERBACK
MAKES THIS IN
EVERY HUDDLE.

Now arrange the circled letters to form
the surprise answer, as suggested by the
above cartoon.

Print
answer
here: A

Unscramble these four Jumbles, one letter to each square, to form four ordinary words.

RYPEK

SHOAC

CITOXE

UPDELD

I've got some great shots, boss

Get them developed

EDITOR

WHAT THE NEW PHOTOGRAPHER SOUGHT FOR HIS WORK.

Now arrange the circled letters to form the surprise answer, as suggested by the above cartoon.

Print answer here:

JUMBLE®

Unscramble these four Jumbles, one letter to
each square, to form four ordinary words.

FYLOT

SHEWO

DIZAWR

JANGOR

This robe is warm and comfy

THIS HELPS
WHEN WORKING
ON A HOME
COMPUTER.

Now arrange the circled letters to form
the surprise answer, as suggested by the
above cartoon.

Print answer here: " ◯◯◯◯ " – ◯◯◯◯

JUMBLE®

Unscramble these four Jumbles, one letter to
each square, to form four ordinary words.

INVEG

KANOE

TIPIED

SLAFTE

This will create a peaceful,
yet colorful setting

WHAT A CREA-
TIVE GARDENER
LIKES TO DO.

Now arrange the circled letters to form
the surprise answer, as suggested by the
above cartoon.

Print answer here:

JUMBLE.

Unscramble these four Jumbles, one letter to
each square, to form four ordinary words.

INARG

RAFIR

MISTEK

LEUXED

She's a
knockout

And talented, too

HOW HE DE-
SCRIBED THE
SHAPELY GIRL AT
THE ICE RINK.

Now arrange the circled letters to form
the surprise answer, as suggested by the
above cartoon.

Print
answer
here:

A " ⬡⬡⬡⬡⬡⬡ " ⬡⬡⬡⬡⬡

JUMBLE®

Unscramble these four Jumbles, one letter to each square, to form four ordinary words.

TOHRT

HYSOW

DUCLOY

CRONAR

That was rougher than a blind side hit

WHAT THE FOOT-BALL TEAM EXPERIENCED AFTER A BUMPY FLIGHT.

Now arrange the circled letters to form the surprise answer, as suggested by the above cartoon.

Print answer here: A ☐☐☐☐☐ ☐☐☐☐

91

JUMBLE®

Unscramble these four Jumbles, one letter to
each square, to form four ordinary words.

VALAR

KICHT

WARBOR

NUCCOR

What a great
getaway

Can I get you
a drink?

EMPLOYEES ON
A CRUISE SHIP
DO THIS ALL
THE TIME.

Now arrange the circled letters to form
the surprise answer, as suggested by the
above cartoon.

Print
answer
here:

ON
A

JUMBLE®

Unscramble these four Jumbles, one letter to each square, to form four ordinary words.

TEELI

BUAQS

TOCIPE

TENNIT

This doesn't work

COMPLAINTS DEP'T

Everything is garbled

My bill is wrong

WHAT THE IRATE CUSTOMERS GAVE THE PHONE COMPANY.

Now arrange the circled letters to form the surprise answer, as suggested by the above cartoon.

Print answer here: A ⬡⬡⬡ OF ⬡⬡⬡⬡⬡⬡⬡

JUMBLE®

Unscramble these four Jumbles, one letter to each square, to form four ordinary words.

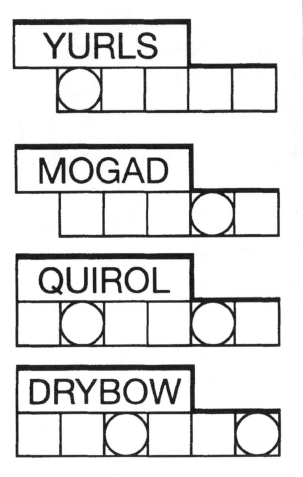

YURLS

MOGAD

QUIROL

DRYBOW

Mind if I get ahead of you?

SOMETHING A WISE GUY USUALLY LACKS.

Now arrange the circled letters to form the surprise answer, as suggested by the above cartoon.

Print answer here:

Unscramble these four Jumbles, one letter to each square, to form four ordinary words.

NORDE

BITHA

DWEAMO

NAANAB

THE CENSORED LOONIES

WHAT THE OUT-RAGEOUS ROCK GROUP BECAME.

Now arrange the circled letters to form the surprise answer, as suggested by the above cartoon.

Print answer here: A

JUMBLE®

Unscramble these four Jumbles, one letter to
each square, to form four ordinary words.

HOCEK

TILAP

LAISOR

AGMENT

ONE TOO MANY
DRINKS CAUSED
HIM TO DO
THIS.

Now arrange the circled letters to form
the surprise answer, as suggested by the
above cartoon.

Print answer here: ◯◯◯◯◯ " ◯◯◯◯◯ "

JUMBLE®

Unscramble these four Jumbles, one letter to each square, to form four ordinary words.

TIARE

ENPAC

GARAVE

NATTEX

Fascinating

How's the needle feel?

WATCHING THE TATTOO ARTIST BECAME THIS.

Now arrange the circled letters to form the surprise answer, as suggested by the above cartoon.

Print answer here:

Unscramble these four Jumbles, one letter to
each square, to form four ordinary words.

AMGUT

SHURC

FAHBLE

LICTIE

WHAT A HAUNTED
HOUSE BECOMES
ON HALLOWEEN.

Now arrange the circled letters to form
the surprise answer, as suggested by the
above cartoon.

Print answer here: A ☐☐☐☐☐☐ ☐☐☐☐

Unscramble these four Jumbles, one letter to
each square, to form four ordinary words.

CAFTE

TESCA

CHAPER

CLOSIA

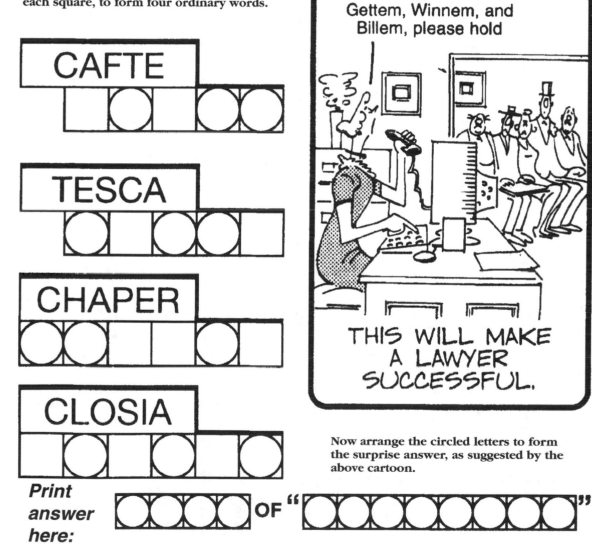

Gettem, Winnem, and
Billem, please hold

THIS WILL MAKE
A LAWYER
SUCCESSFUL.

Now arrange the circled letters to form
the surprise answer, as suggested by the
above cartoon.

Print answer here: ◯◯◯◯◯ OF "◯◯◯◯◯◯◯◯◯"

Unscramble these four Jumbles, one letter to each square, to form four ordinary words.

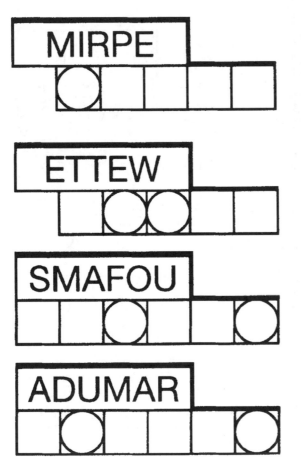

MIRPE

ETTEW

SMAFOU

ADUMAR

Got him

I'm hungry and thirsty and this won't end

EASY TO FEEL LIKE THIS WORKING IN THE EVERGLADES.

Now arrange the circled letters to form the surprise answer, as suggested by the above cartoon.

Print answer here:

JUMBLE®

Unscramble these four Jumbles, one letter to each square, to form four ordinary words.

MAIDT

RAHME

DOUBEY

GOUHNE

Uh oh, they're here again

NO MORE KILLING

SAVE THE WILDLIFE

WHAT THE ANIMAL RIGHTS GROUP DID TO THE FOX HUNTERS.

Now arrange the circled letters to form the surprise answer, as suggested by the above cartoon.

Print answer here: ⬡⬡⬡⬡⬡⬡⬡ ⬡⬡⬡⬡

101

Unscramble these four Jumbles, one letter to each square, to form four ordinary words.

WICTE

HYNIS

KOPHOU

FLOUBE

No, it was my pleasure

WHEN THE ROOFER PITCHED IN TO HELP HIS NEIGH-BOR, IT WAS--

Now arrange the circled letters to form the surprise answer, as suggested by the above cartoon.

Print answer here: ⬡⬡ ⬡⬡⬡ ⬡⬡⬡⬡⬡

JUMBLE®

Unscramble these four Jumbles, one letter to each square, to form four ordinary words.

THYFE

GINTY

DINGHI

GENNIE

FREE MEALS WITH ROOM

PAY ONCE, STAY TWICE

WHAT THE COMPETING HOTEL OWNERS GOT INVOLVED IN.

Now arrange the circled letters to form the surprise answer, as suggested by the above cartoon.

Print answer here:

Unscramble these four Jumbles, one letter to
each square, to form four ordinary words.

VIPTO
◯◯□◯

ELLIS
□□◯◯◯

TESHEE
◯□□◯□□

PREMAT
□□□◯◯◯

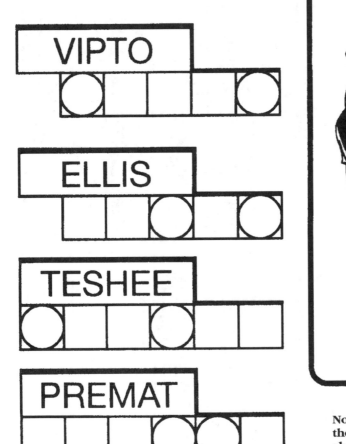

Next, cut frame
to fit area

THE BEST WAY
TO BUILD A
STAIRCASE WITH
A DO-IT-
YOURSELF KIT.

Now arrange the circled letters to form
the surprise answer, as suggested by the
above cartoon.

Print answer here: ◯◯◯◯ BY ◯◯◯◯

JUMBLE®

Unscramble these four Jumbles, one letter to each square, to form four ordinary words.

CANYF

ANUDT

INREEM

CEERUD

HE GOT THE JOB AS A PIANO MOVER ALTHOUGH HE COULDN'T EVEN DO THIS.

Now arrange the circled letters to form the surprise answer, as suggested by the above cartoon.

Print answer here: ◯◯◯◯◯ A ◯◯◯◯

JUMBLE®

Unscramble these four Jumbles, one letter to
each square, to form four ordinary words.

EVIRT

NOCOL

PINGAY

STYLUB

Hurry up, you're running late

A HARD WORKING
GARBAGE MAN
DOESN'T MIND
WHEN HIS BOSS
DOES THIS.

Now arrange the circled letters to form
the surprise answer, as suggested by the
above cartoon.

Print answer here:

JUMBLE®

Unscramble these four Jumbles, one letter to each square, to form four ordinary words.

REZIP

⬜⬜⬜⬜⬜

EYAPE

⬜⬜⬜⬜

KROMES

⬜⬜⬜⬜⬜⬜

GLAHGE

⬜⬜⬜⬜⬜⬜

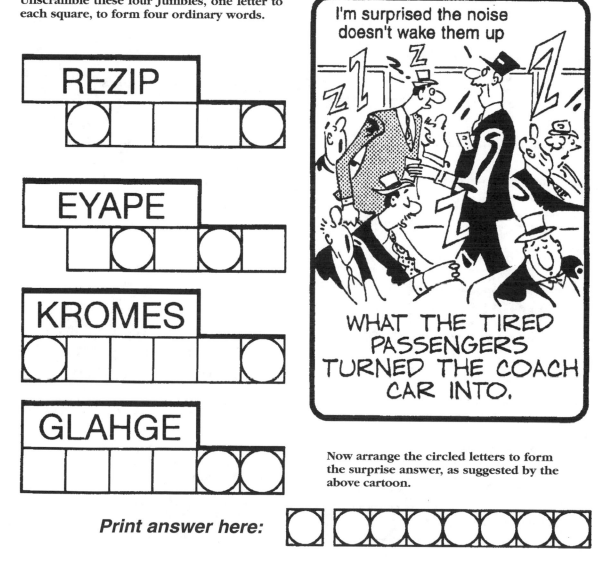

I'm surprised the noise doesn't wake them up

WHAT THE TIRED PASSENGERS TURNED THE COACH CAR INTO.

Now arrange the circled letters to form the surprise answer, as suggested by the above cartoon.

Print answer here: ⬜ ⬜⬜⬜⬜⬜⬜⬜

JUMBLE®

Unscramble these four Jumbles, one letter to
each square, to form four ordinary words.

BRUTS
◯◯◯☐☐

LOTEX
◯☐☐◯◯

RYCKIT
◯◯☐◯☐☐

THUBOG
☐◯◯☐☐◯

You're late!   Sorry, your Honor

THE LAWYER DIDN'T
WANT TO DO THIS
DURING THE TRIAL.

Now arrange the circled letters to form
the surprise answer, as suggested by the
above cartoon.

Print answer here: ◯◯◯◯◯ ◯◯◯◯◯◯◯

JUMBLE®

Unscramble these four Jumbles, one letter to
each square, to form four ordinary words.

ATQUO

UGLID

SAURES

COMIAT

A CHIMNEY SWEEP
WEARS THIS
TO WORK.

Now arrange the circled letters to form
the surprise answer, as suggested by the
above cartoon.

Print answer here: A ⬡⬡⬡⬡⬡ ⬡⬡⬡⬡

JUMBLE®

Unscramble these four Jumbles, one letter to each square, to form four ordinary words.

SEMYS

SUJOT

KERROB

VIKONE

You live on top of a wooded hill

How did you know?

WHAT SHE CON-SIDERED THE FORTUNE TELLER.

Now arrange the circled letters to form the surprise answer, as suggested by the above cartoon.

Print answer here: A

110

Unscramble these four Jumbles, one letter to each square, to form four ordinary words.

RYVEN

CHABT

MOUPID

SUPCAM

A GOOD WAY TO RELAX ON THE WEEKEND.

Now arrange the circled letters to form the surprise answer, as suggested by the above cartoon.

Print answer here: ⬡⬡⬡⬡⬡ THE ⬡⬡⬡⬡⬡

JUMBLE®

Unscramble these four Jumbles, one letter to
each square, to form four ordinary words.

TANCH

LABAN

VERYUP

PRAMCE

Strange creatures,
aren't they?

WHAT THE ANI-
MALS ENJOYED
WATCHING.

Now arrange the circled letters to form
the surprise answer, as suggested by the
above cartoon.

Print answer here: THE ◯◯◯◯◯ ◯◯◯◯

Unscramble these four Jumbles, one letter to each square, to form four ordinary words.

FINEK

TIXSY

LUFTAY

CUROGH

Good job, but pick up the pace

FURNITURE

UPHOLSTERING A CHAIR CAN BE THIS.

Now arrange the circled letters to form the surprise answer, as suggested by the above cartoon.

Print answer here: " ◯◯◯◯◯ - ◯◯◯ " **WORK**

JUMBLE®

Unscramble these four Jumbles, one letter to
each square, to form four ordinary words.

ETHUC

INCCY

MESECH

SMAJET

WHAT MOM EN-
JOYED WHILE
DOING THE
LINENS.

Now arrange the circled letters to form
the surprise answer, as suggested by the
above cartoon.

Print answer here: "◯◯◯◯◯" ◯◯◯◯◯◯

JUMBLE®

Unscramble these four Jumbles, one letter to each square, to form four ordinary words.

KRYJE

NOANY

SAYILE

LYNKIG

You look fabulous

The secret is small portions

IMPORTANT TO KNOW BEFORE TRYING THE NEW FAD DIET.

Now arrange the circled letters to form the surprise answer, as suggested by the above cartoon.

Print answer here: THE ⬡⬡⬡⬡⬡⬡⬡

JUMBLE®

Unscramble these four Jumbles, one letter to each square, to form four ordinary words.

HOACC

HURTT

YAIRPT

UFTOIT

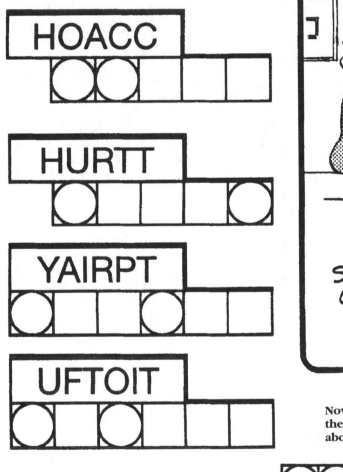

No relief in sight

STEAMY WEATHER CAN TURN INTO THIS ON THE NEWS.

Now arrange the circled letters to form the surprise answer, as suggested by the above cartoon.

Print answer here: A

JUMBLE.

Unscramble these four Jumbles, one letter to each square, to form four ordinary words.

WARLD
◯◯◯ ◯◯

RINGO
□□ ◯◯◯

MUDINS
◯◯◯ ◯◯◯

GOSPEN
◯□□□ ◯◯

This is not the weekend, Jones

THE RESULT OF WEARING CASUAL CLOTHES TO A FORMAL MEETING.

Now arrange the circled letters to form the surprise answer, as suggested by the above cartoon.

Print answer here: A ◯◯◯◯◯◯◯◯ ◯◯◯◯

JUMBLE®

Unscramble these four Jumbles, one letter to each square, to form four ordinary words.

CHARP

FELCT

BOBJER

NEPOTT

That looks nicer than my place

BUILDING A DOG HOUSE FOR FIDO TURNED INTO THIS.

Now arrange the circled letters to form the surprise answer, as suggested by the above cartoon.

Print answer here: A

118

JUMBLE®

Unscramble these four Jumbles, one letter to
each square, to form four ordinary words.

NOFEL

PLUJE

TOBUNT

CAFFEE

Never touch it

SHE DOESN'T
DRINK COFFEE
BECAUSE IT'S----

Now arrange the circled letters to form
the surprise answer, as suggested by the
above cartoon.

Print answer here: ◯◯◯ HER ◯◯◯ OF ◯◯◯

119

JUMBLE®

Unscramble these four Jumbles, one letter to each square, to form four ordinary words.

LOPNY

TAUDI

GINOUT

TIFFUL

A new record

This makes me feel good

WHAT THE MUSCLE MAN CONSIDERED HIS VICTORY.

Now arrange the circled letters to form the surprise answer, as suggested by the above cartoon.

Print answer here:

Unscramble these four Jumbles, one letter to each square, to form four ordinary words.

PIMBL

HOPOW

IMMORE

AMRUTE

Where were we?

THE ABSENT-MINDED PRO-FESSOR HAD PLENTY OF THIS.

Now arrange the circled letters to form the surprise answer, as suggested by the above cartoon.

Print answer here: ⬭⬭⬭⬭⬭ **AT THE** ⬭⬭⬭

JUMBLE

Unscramble these four Jumbles, one letter to each square, to form four ordinary words.

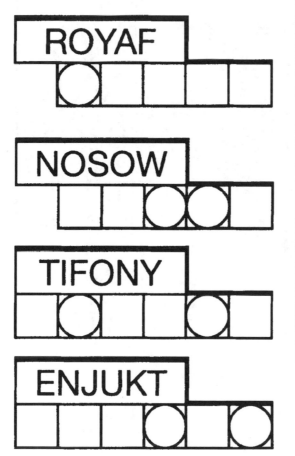

ROYAF

NOSOW

TIFONY

ENJUKT

He'll be a Colonel in no time

THIS HAPPENED TO HIS CAREER WHEN HE BE-CAME A PILOT.

Now arrange the circled letters to form the surprise answer, as suggested by the above cartoon.

Print answer here: IT ◯◯◯◯ ◯◯◯

Unscramble these four Jumbles, one letter to
each square, to form four ordinary words.

WELJE

RUTYL

HASFIM

FLIEBE

WHAT THE CAMERA-
MAN CAPTURED ON
HIS PHOTO OF
MOONSHINERS.

Now arrange the circled letters to form
the surprise answer, as suggested by the
above cartoon.

Print answer here: A " ⬡⬡⬡⬡⬡ " ⬡⬡⬡⬡

Unscramble these four Jumbles, one letter to each square, to form four ordinary words.

DAGEA

ROSYR

KENASH

WEFURC

I can't get this to work

Don't worry, you'll get it

WHY THE LOCK-SMITH'S COM-PUTER DIDN'T WORK.

Now arrange the circled letters to form the surprise answer, as suggested by the above cartoon.

Print answer here:

HE ☐☐☐☐ THE ☐☐☐☐☐ ☐☐☐

Unscramble these four Jumbles, one letter to each square, to form four ordinary words.

HAKSY

YASTT

MARKEB

KOJECY

WHEN IT COMES TO CONTESTS HER DESSERT DOES THIS.

Now arrange the circled letters to form the surprise answer, as suggested by the above cartoon.

Print answer here: ⬡⬡⬡⬡⬡ **THE** ⬡⬡⬡⬡

JUMBLE®

Unscramble these four Jumbles, one letter to each square, to form four ordinary words.

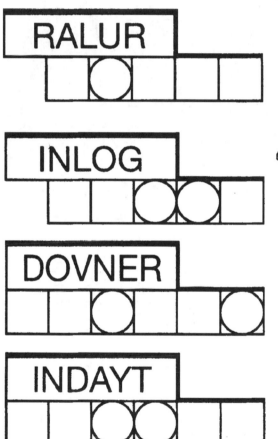

RALUR

INLOG

DOVNER

INDAYT

VOTE FOR ME

WHAT THE SUC-
CESSFUL POLITI-
CIAN EXCELLED AT.

Now arrange the circled letters to form the surprise answer, as suggested by the above cartoon.

Print answer here:

Unscramble these four Jumbles, one letter to each square, to form four ordinary words.

HAWRT

YIEPT

YENNIT

GOUTUD

TUITION

YOU ARE USUALLY REQUIRED TO PAY THIS IN COLLEGE.

Now arrange the circled letters to form the surprise answer, as suggested by the above cartoon.

Print answer here:

Unscramble these four Jumbles, one letter to each square, to form four ordinary words.

KYDUS

TACCH

ENTAUB

TUCLED

Sorry, fellas--I'll have to downsize the operation

WHAT THE BOSS DID WHEN BUSINESS GOT SLOW.

Now arrange the circled letters to form the surprise answer, as suggested by the above cartoon.

Print answer here:

128

Unscramble these four Jumbles, one letter to
each square, to form four ordinary words.

CELEX

ROAPE

GLABEN

NYLKID

I can't wait till
my shift ends

HOW THE
HOLIDAY GIFT—
WRAPPER FELT.

Now arrange the circled letters to form
the surprise answer, as suggested by the
above cartoon.

Print answer here:

129

JUMBLE®

Unscramble these four Jumbles, one letter to each square, to form four ordinary words.

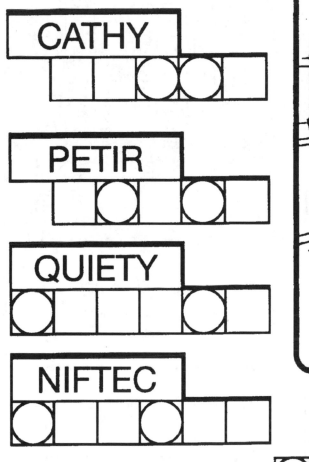

CATHY

PETIR

QUIETY

NIFTEC

THIS CAN BE TOUGH WHEN THE MEAT IS TENDER.

Now arrange the circled letters to form the surprise answer, as suggested by the above cartoon.

Print answer here:

JUMBLE®

Unscramble these four Jumbles, one letter to each square, to form four ordinary words.

RYTAR

LUNCE

EMBACE

DOURNA

Very successful sale

WHAT THE GROCER GOT WHEN HE LOWERED THE PRICE ON DETERGENT.

Now arrange the circled letters to form the surprise answer, as suggested by the above cartoon.

Print answer here:

131

JUMBLE®

Unscramble these four Jumbles, one letter to each square, to form four ordinary words.

RODUG

HAGUL

REYYAL

LYBBAF

WHAT CHRISTMAS IS FOR MANY.

Now arrange the circled letters to form the surprise answer, as suggested by the above cartoon.

Print answer here: A ☐☐☐☐☐ ☐☐☐

Unscramble these four Jumbles, one letter to each square, to form four ordinary words.

RINBY

USVEA

YIPLOC

EDDOCE

He's hiding something

WHAT THE CROOKED POLITICIAN WAS INVOLVED IN WHEN HE PAINTED HIS OFFICE.

Now arrange the circled letters to form the surprise answer, as suggested by the above cartoon.

Print answer here: A ⭕⭕⭕⭕⭕ ⭕⭕

Unscramble these four Jumbles, one letter to
each square, to form four ordinary words.

UNAFA

DYNBA

ELBARR

ELCHEK

This has got to stop!

BELT TIGHTENING
CALLS FOR THIS.

Now arrange the circled letters to form
the surprise answer, as suggested by the
above cartoon.

Print answer here: A ◯◯◯◯◯◯

Unscramble these four Jumbles, one letter to each square, to form four ordinary words.

TURTE

GOSUB

WHERDS

TONPHY

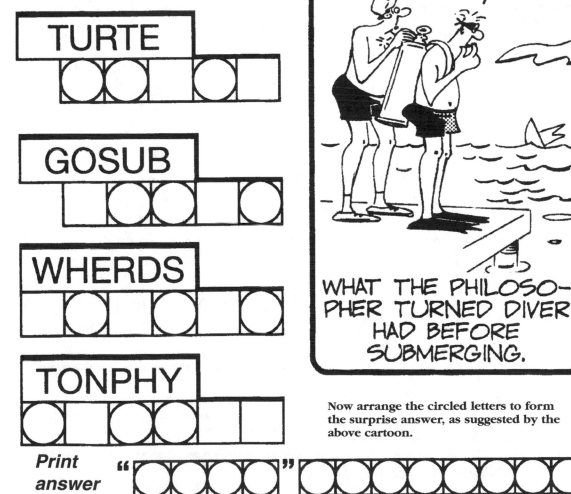

How far down is it?

WHAT THE PHILOSO-
PHER TURNED DIVER
HAD BEFORE
SUBMERGING.

Now arrange the circled letters to form the surprise answer, as suggested by the above cartoon.

Print answer here: " ⬡⬡⬡⬡ " ⬡⬡⬡⬡⬡⬡⬡⬡⬡

JUMBLE®

Unscramble these four Jumbles, one letter to each square, to form four ordinary words.

REMEG

NAIRY

TIDOAR

MILDIP

They signed a pre-nuptial agreement

THIS WILL AVOID ALIMONY.

Now arrange the circled letters to form the surprise answer, as suggested by the above cartoon.

Print answer here:

Unscramble these four Jumbles, one letter to each square, to form four ordinary words.

NORST

GUBYL

LOCCIA

REBAWE

No shade and I'm out $50

WHAT SHE DID WHEN THE WIND BROKE HER BEACH UMBRELLA.

Now arrange the circled letters to form the surprise answer, as suggested by the above cartoon.

Print answer here: A ◯◯◯◯ ◯◯◯◯

JUMBLE®

Unscramble these four Jumbles, one letter to
each square, to form four ordinary words.

OPSOW

NATEC

TAUROH

RAXLYN

Let's grab
a sandwich

Haven't got
time

A NOON-TIME
WORKOUT CAN
TURN INTO THIS.

Now arrange the circled letters to form
the surprise answer, as suggested by the
above cartoon.

**Print answer
here:** A " ⬡⬡⬡⬡⬡ " ⬡⬡⬡⬡⬡⬡

JUMBLE®

Unscramble these four Jumbles, one letter to
each square, to form four ordinary words.

BUICC

STRUY

LOSFIS

KRANET

I'll hem
it below
the knee

Aw, Mom, that's
too long

A GOOD WAY TO
COMPLY WITH A
SCHOOL DRESS
CODE.

Now arrange the circled letters to form
the surprise answer, as suggested by the
above cartoon.

**Print answer
here:** ⃝⃝⃝⃝⃝ THE ⃝⃝⃝⃝⃝

JUMBLE®

Unscramble these four Jumbles, one letter to each square, to form four ordinary words.

FRIGE

REFIA

INBOUN

LABERV

WHOA!!

That nag knows who's boss

WHEN THE KING TAMED THE WILD HORSE HE PROVED THAT HE WAS----

Now arrange the circled letters to form the surprise answer, as suggested by the above cartoon.

Print answer here: THE " ⬡⬡⬡⬡⬡⬡⬡ " ⬡⬡⬡⬡⬡

Unscramble these four Jumbles, one letter to each square, to form four ordinary words.

GLEEY

OTTOH

ROCTAV

SUNDAI

Wow! 100% in math!

Extra credit for neatness

A PERSON WHO MAKES LITTLE THINGS COUNT.

Now arrange the circled letters to form the surprise answer, as suggested by the above cartoon.

Print answer here: A ◯◯◯◯◯◯◯

141

JUMBLE®

Unscramble these four Jumbles, one letter to each square, to form four ordinary words.

DESET

TRAIE

NERUNG

WARMOR

Hey — wanna get killed?!

SCREECH!

WHAT JAYWALKERS MAY BE WEARING TOMORROW.

Now arrange the circled letters to form the surprise answer, as suggested by the above cartoon.

Print answer here: ⟨○○○○○⟩

142

JUMBLE®

Unscramble these four Jumbles, one letter to each square, to form four ordinary words.

ANCOP

DRAIP

MUDINS

LEMITY

Sure loves himself

WHAT THE EGOTIST WAS SUFFERING FROM.

Now arrange the circled letters to form the surprise answer, as suggested by the above cartoon.

Print answer here: " ⬚ " ⬚⬚⬚⬚⬚⬚

JUMBLE®

Unscramble these four Jumbles, one letter to each square, to form four ordinary words.

SYKAH

RODAH

IMVOTE

STEJER

WHAT THE CUTE LITTLE POTATO WAS WARNED AGAINST.

Now arrange the circled letters to form the surprise answer, as suggested by the above cartoon.

Print answer here:

Unscramble these four Jumbles, one letter to each square, to form four ordinary words.

SOMYS

RUGPO

GORUME

THEIRE

WHAT BOARDING HOUSE GOSSIP USED TO START WITH.

Now arrange the circled letters to form the surprise answer, as suggested by the above cartoon.

Print answer here: " ⬡⬡⬡⬡⬡⬡⬡ "

Unscramble these four Jumbles, one letter to
each square, to form four ordinary words.

ASOBS

MORRA

KALTEC

CUSTOC

WHAT THE
TWELVE BOTTLES OF
MOONSHINE EVENTUALLY
BECAME.

Now arrange the circled letters to form
the surprise answer, as suggested by the
above cartoon.

Print answer here: A ⬡⬡⬡⬡⬡ ⬡⬡⬡⬡

JUMBLE®

Unscramble these four Jumbles, one letter to each square, to form four ordinary words.

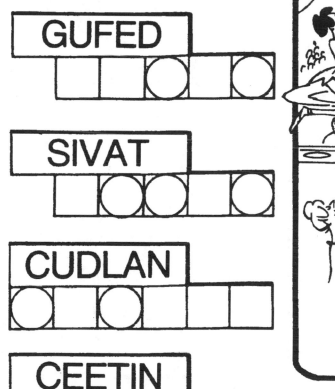

GUFED

SIVAT

CUDLAN

CEETIN

RATHER BIG
FOR BALLET
THESE DAYS.

Now arrange the circled letters to form the surprise answer, as suggested by the above cartoon.

Print answer here:

147

JUMBLE®

Unscramble these four Jumbles, one letter to
each square, to form four ordinary words.

TUMON

FLYIM

FRINIM

YAXLAG

Your
steak,
sir

WHAT HORSEMEAT
IS TO A DOG.

Now arrange the circled letters to form
the surprise answer, as suggested by the
above cartoon.

Print
answer
here: " ☐☐☐☐☐ " ☐☐☐☐☐☐

JUMBLE®

Unscramble these four Jumbles, one letter to
each square, to form four ordinary words.

AMELY

SUGES

YUPRIF

INLATE

WE CLOSE OUR
EYES TO THIS.

Now arrange the circled letters to form
the surprise answer, as suggested by the
above cartoon.

Print answer here:

149

Unscramble these four Jumbles, one letter to each square, to form four ordinary words.

PLIMB

BYBOH

ENBLIM

GRANDO

Stand still!

WHERE THE OVER-ZEALOUS COW GAVE HER MILK.

Now arrange the circled letters to form the surprise answer, as suggested by the above cartoon.

Print answer here:

⬡⬡⬡⬡⬡⬡ THE " ⬡⬡⬡⬡ "

Unscramble these four Jumbles, one letter to each square, to form four ordinary words.

BAITH

AMDAM

GRATUI

LAMORF

Don't forget the ketchup

SOMEONE WHO RAIDS THE REFRIGERATOR FOR A MIDNIGHT SNACK.

Now arrange the circled letters to form the surprise answer, as suggested by the above cartoon.

Print answer here: " ☐☐☐ - ☐☐☐☐☐☐☐ "

151

JUMBLE®

Unscramble these four Jumbles, one letter to
each square, to form four ordinary words.

GLOIN
◯☐☐☐☐

NUWDE
◯☐☐☐☐

MIRTHE
◯☐☐☐☐☐

YORCAN
◯☐☐☐☐◯

IT'S USUAL TO
HAVE THIS BEFORE
DINNER.

Now arrange the circled letters to form
the surprise answer, as suggested by the
above cartoon.

Print answer here: ◯◯◯◯◯

JUMBLE®

Unscramble these four Jumbles, one letter to each square, to form four ordinary words.

EWLEH

REMEB

IBINIK

RANLYX

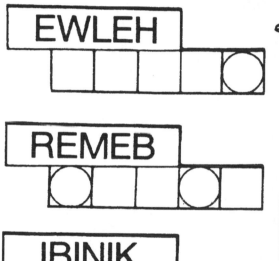

See ya
around

WHAT THE TRAVELING CORRESPONDENT'S WIFE DIDN'T LIKE.

Now arrange the circled letters to form the surprise answer, as suggested by the above cartoon.

Print answer here: HIS " ☐☐☐ ☐☐☐☐ "

JUMBLE®

Unscramble these four Jumbles, one letter to
each square, to form four ordinary words.

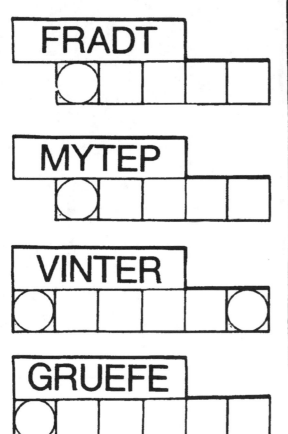

FRADT

MYTEP

VINTER

GRUEFE

YOU CAN ALWAYS
GROW THIS IN YOUR
GARDEN IF YOU WORK
HARD ENOUGH.

Now arrange the circled letters to form
the surprise answer, as suggested by the
above cartoon.

Print answer here:

JUMBLE®

Unscramble these four Jumbles, one letter to each square, to form four ordinary words.

MUIBE

HOCEK

GALENT

BOYDUL

SOMETHING BESIDES THE TIDE WHICH THE MOON AFFECTS.

Now arrange the circled letters to form the surprise answer, as suggested by the above cartoon.

Print answer here: THE ⬡⬡⬡⬡⬡⬡

Unscramble these four Jumbles, one letter to each square, to form four ordinary words.

WROCE

PUJEL

BLITAR

MAINEA

HAIRCUT $40
SHAVE $20
SHAMPOO $30

WHAT YOU MIGHT CALL THIS BARBER'S ESTABLISHMENT.

Now arrange the circled letters to form the surprise answer, as suggested by the above cartoon.

Print answer here: A ⬜⬜⬜⬜⬜ ⬜⬜⬜⬜⬜⬜

Unscramble these four Jumbles, one letter to each square, to form four ordinary words.

DEROO

VORAF

HYRITT

LIRBED

The world's gone to pot

The end can't be far off

WHAT SHE CALLED HER SOURPUSS HUSBAND.

Now arrange the circled letters to form the surprise answer, as suggested by the above cartoon.

Print answer here: HER ⬡⬡⬡⬡⬡⬡ ⬡⬡⬡⬡

157

Unscramble these four Jumbles, one letter to each square, to form four ordinary words.

OVERP

TIFED

BINLEB

GROINI

How about a date, beautiful?

THE BOXER'S SMOOTH LINE FINALLY GOT HIM THIS.

Now arrange the circled letters to form the surprise answer, as suggested by the above cartoon.

Print answer here:

PUZZLE 157

Unscramble these four Jumbles, one letter to each square, to form four ordinary words.

ROGAC

FINEK

TIPPEC

TINKTE

A MAN WHOSE WORK REQUIRES HIM TO GRASP THINGS QUICKLY.

Now arrange the circled letters to form the surprise answer, as suggested by the above cartoon.

Print answer here: A ⭘⭘⭘⭘⭘⭘⭘⭘⭘⭘⭘

159

JUMBLE®

Unscramble these four Jumbles, one letter to each square, to form four ordinary words.

ROGOM

MYOFA

UNCANE

SELING

WHAT HER EARNINGS OFTEN DON'T KEEP UP WITH.

Fine Jewelry

Now arrange the circled letters to form the surprise answer, as suggested by the above cartoon.

Print answer here: HER

JUMBLE®

Unscramble these four Jumbles, one letter to each square, to form four ordinary words.

VALIE

FONTE

REDDEG

UMSCAP

WHAT THE SAILOR BECAME WHEN HE MARRIED A WIDOW.

Now arrange the circled letters to form the surprise answer, as suggested by the above cartoon.

Print answer here: A

Unscramble these four Jumbles, one letter to each square, to form four ordinary words.

LUCOT

MALUB

AFDACE

GOHEAM

We'll be toasty warm in here soon

WHAT IT TAKES TO GET THESE TWO ALL FIRED UP.

Now arrange the circled letters to form the surprise answer, as suggested by the above cartoon.

Print answer here:

JUMBLE®

Mania

Challenger Puzzles

JUMBLE®

Unscramble these six Jumbles, one letter to each square, to form six ordinary words.

DORCEF

TEENAG

SEBIED

WOCALL

BEJOCT

FLOANG

Had to go to my great-grandmother's funeral

HE GOT FIRED FROM HIS JOB FOR LYING---

Now arrange the circled letters to form the surprise answer, as suggested by the above cartoon.

PRINT YOUR ANSWER IN THE CIRCLES BELOW

164

JUMBLE®

Unscramble these six Jumbles, one letter to each square, to form six ordinary words.

RANOUD

GICART

MULASY

HERBTO

GROANJ

AGOVEY

HIS MOTHER-IN-LAW'S SHORTCOMING WAS THIS.

Now arrange the circled letters to form the surprise answer, as suggested by the above cartoon.

PRINT YOUR ANSWER IN THE CIRCLES BELOW

HER " ⬡⬡⬡⬡⬡ ⬡⬡⬡⬡⬡⬡⬡ "

JUMBLE®

Unscramble these six Jumbles, one letter to each square, to form six ordinary words.

MOYPLE

SICCEN

NAANAB

TRUGET

CAVELE

EMSIDE

THE FIRST DUTY OF THE MISSIONARY WAS TO CONVERT THE CANNIBALS TO THIS.

Now arrange the circled letters to form the surprise answer, as suggested by the above cartoon.

PRINT YOUR ANSWER IN THE CIRCLES BELOW

JUMBLE®

Unscramble these six Jumbles, one letter to each square, to form six ordinary words.

MUSCLY

BRATIL

CACTEN

LOOBER

YURELS

RAZTUQ

THE KIND OF PEOPLE YOU MIGHT MEET AT THE INFORMATION BUREAU.

Now arrange the circled letters to form the surprise answer, as suggested by the above cartoon.

PRINT YOUR ANSWER IN THE CIRCLES BELOW

" ◯◯◯◯◯◯◯◯◯◯◯◯◯ " ONES

JUMBLE®

Unscramble these six Jumbles, one letter to each square, to form six ordinary words.

SERJEY

FUPULC

LAPLID

DORNEV

ZEABAL

ABNOME

This should get him to make up his mind

POST OFFICE

You're right, Mom

WHAT THAT LOVE LETTER WAS CALCULATED TO DO.

Now arrange the circled letters to form the surprise answer, as suggested by the above cartoon.

PRINT YOUR ANSWER IN THE CIRCLES BELOW

THE " "

JUMBLE®

Unscramble these six Jumbles, one letter to each square, to form six ordinary words.

EMBLAG

DINTUC

PACALA

NOOTIL

CAFEDE

YINCLE

Always boasting

NOTHING GETS A PERSON ALL UP IN THE AIR QUICKER THAN THIS.

Now arrange the circled letters to form the surprise answer, as suggested by the above cartoon.

PRINT YOUR ANSWER IN THE CIRCLES BELOW

JUMBLE®

Unscramble these six Jumbles, one letter to each square, to form six ordinary words.

LOMOGY

VORCLE

NIVERM

BLOGIE

EATREA

YEWARL

Brr–it's cold in here

THAT ANCIENT STATUE PHONED HIS INSURANCE BROKER BECAUSE HE NEEDED THIS.

Now arrange the circled letters to form the surprise answer, as suggested by the above cartoon.

PRINT YOUR ANSWER IN THE CIRCLES BELOW

◯◯◯◯◯ "◯◯◯◯◯◯◯◯◯"

JUMBLE®

Unscramble these six Jumbles, one letter to
each square, to form six ordinary words.

PARREY

WEREVS

LAYMIN

PERICH

SMILFY

ICETOX

HOME COOKING IS
WHAT A MAN
MISSES WHEN THIS
HAPPENS.

Now arrange the circled letters to form
the surprise answer, as suggested by the
above cartoon.

PRINT YOUR ANSWER IN THE CIRCLES BELOW

◯◯◯ ◯◯◯◯◯ ◯◯◯◯'◯

171

JUMBLE®

Unscramble these six Jumbles, one letter to
each square, to form six ordinary words.

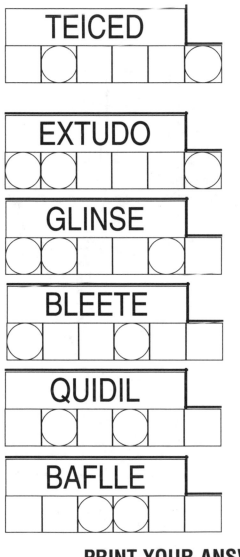

TEICED

EXTUDO

GLINSE

BLEETE

QUIDIL

BAFLLE

I brought the agenda

IMPORTANT
FOR HER
BUSINESS LUNCH.

Now arrange the circled letters to form
the surprise answer, as suggested by the
above cartoon.

PRINT YOUR ANSWER IN THE CIRCLES BELOW

A "〇〇〇〇〇 - 〇〇〇〇〇   〇〇〇〇〇〇〇"

JUMBLE®

Unscramble these six Jumbles, one letter to each square, to form six ordinary words.

LIMBEN

THUNGA

STABEK

SCONED

YARNEL

SCEBIT

How does he do that?

THE ART OF MAGIC IS ---

Now arrange the circled letters to form the surprise answer, as suggested by the above cartoon.

PRINT YOUR ANSWER IN THE CIRCLES BELOW

A

JUMBLE®

Unscramble these six Jumbles, one letter to each square, to form six ordinary words.

FLEMUF

SLUHBE

KNIBAG

TAUMUN

INLARM

ARIDAL

SOME DERMATOL-OGISTS OFTEN DO THIS.

Now arrange the circled letters to form the surprise answer, as suggested by the above cartoon.

PRINT YOUR ANSWER IN THE CIRCLES BELOW

YOUR

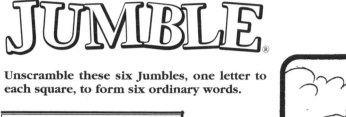

Unscramble these six Jumbles, one letter to each square, to form six ordinary words.

DECLUD

GEELUM

YEMINT

STIGAR

FEXPIR

BRUNAU

Let's pool our money

WHAT THE FINAN-CIERS INVESTED IN AT THE RACETRACK.

Now arrange the circled letters to form the surprise answer, as suggested by the above cartoon.

PRINT YOUR ANSWER IN THE CIRCLES BELOW

A ◯◯◯◯◯ - ◯◯◯◯◯◯◯ ◯◯◯◯◯

Unscramble these six Jumbles, one letter to
each square, to form six ordinary words.

ROOLIE

TENTAX

DOULCY

TAMMOR

SUMPAC

LESUNS

It starts at
$175,000

What's it made
of, GOLD?

WHAT HE CON-
SIDERED THE
EXPENSIVE
SPORTS CAR.

Now arrange the circled letters to form
the surprise answer, as suggested by the
above cartoon.

PRINT YOUR ANSWER IN THE CIRCLES BELOW

JUMBLE®

Unscramble these six Jumbles, one letter to
each square, to form six ordinary words.

NIGMIT

LEENED

NISSIT

SWUNIE

MINGOH

EUMMUS

No distractions up here

Perfect spot

WHY THE STATES-
MEN MET AT A
MOUNTAINTOP
RESORT.

Now arrange the circled letters to form
the surprise answer, as suggested by the
above cartoon.

PRINT YOUR ANSWER IN THE CIRCLES BELOW

FOR
A

JUMBLE®

Unscramble these six Jumbles, one letter to
each square, to form six ordinary words.

UNCOPE

LOICAS

STUJYL

BURMIA

BRUPES

ENTGAM

Let me bait
this for you

I'll show
you how
it's done

ENJOYED BY THE
MOVIE STAR ON
HER FISHING
TRIP.

Now arrange the circled letters to form
the surprise answer, as suggested by the
above cartoon.

PRINT YOUR ANSWER IN THE CIRCLES BELOW

A

JUMBLE®

Unscramble these six Jumbles, one letter to each square, to form six ordinary words.

LIVEEW

ERVEWS

TULTER

KLARET

BLYMAC

DARMIS

Not your best

THE GOLFER TURNED INTO THIS WHEN HIS TEE SHOT WENT ASTRAY.

Now arrange the circled letters to form the surprise answer, as suggested by the above cartoon.

PRINT YOUR ANSWER IN THE CIRCLES BELOW

A

JUMBLE®

Unscramble these six Jumbles, one letter to
each square, to form six ordinary words.

NABYRD

SOUPOR

REECLY

GLIMYR

SHERTH

YEMITS

Shocking!

SCULPTING AN
X-RATED STATUE
MADE HIM THIS.

Now arrange the circled letters to form
the surprise answer, as suggested by the
above cartoon.

PRINT YOUR ANSWER IN THE CIRCLES BELOW

A

PUZZLE
178

JUMBLE®

Unscramble these six Jumbles, one letter to
each square, to form six ordinary words.

TANIAT

INGROI

LIMSAD

TEPROY

PINTUR

YETTIN

This should lead
to a movie role

WHAT THE MODEL
WANTED TO END
UP DOING.

Now arrange the circled letters to form
the surprise answer, as suggested by the
above cartoon.

PRINT YOUR ANSWER IN THE CIRCLES BELOW

JUMBLE®

Unscramble these six Jumbles, one letter to
each square, to form six ordinary words.

BRICKE

CRALIG

CROLIF

DISTEW

NAHDDE

GULJEG

Your resume should
list your degrees

PERSONNEL

OFTEN OBTAINED
FROM A JOB
COUNSELOR.

Now arrange the circled letters to form
the surprise answer, as suggested by the
above cartoon.

PRINT YOUR ANSWER IN THE CIRCLES BELOW

A "◯◯◯◯◯" ◯◯◯◯◯◯◯◯◯

JUMBLE®

Unscramble these six Jumbles, one letter to each square, to form six ordinary words.

NARBEN

BILDOY

SWILEY

REDUME

FREYNI

HUCCOR

They certainly get your attention

WHAT HE DID WHEN SHE BOUGHT HIM GAUDY SUS-PENDERS.

Now arrange the circled letters to form the surprise answer, as suggested by the above cartoon.

PRINT YOUR ANSWER IN THE CIRCLES BELOW

" ⬡⬡⬡⬡⬡⬡ " ⬡⬡⬡⬡⬡⬡⬡⬡

ANSWERS

1. **Jumbles:** BELIE LIMBO UNEASY SURELY
   Answer: What the busy reporter got from his girlfriend—A "BYE" LINE

2. **Jumbles:** LIGHT PROBE INDUCE AMOEBA
   Answer: Some people who don't pay taxes in due time—DO TIME

3. **Jumbles:** NOVEL PURGE MAINLY OBJECT
   Answer: What the guard called the key to the jail, as he threw it away—THE CAN OPENER

4. **Jumbles:** FRAME VISOR COUPON DRUDGE
   Answer: He couldn't think straight because he always had this—CURVES ON HIS MIND

5. **Jumbles:** PEACE HASTY PARISH SPRUCE
   Answer: What you might find in an automobile graveyard—HEAPS OF "HEAPS"

6. **Jumbles:** TOOTH BOGUS INDUCT TRICKY
   Answer: They drank to each other's health so often that this happened—BOTH GOT SICK

7. **Jumbles:** MINOR WAFER ABSORB MOSQUE
   Answer: What briefs are usually "woven" from—"FIBERS"

8. **Jumbles:** RUSTY CHANT FROSTY LAVISH
   Answer: What it turned out to be when they forgot to hook on the dining car—A "FAST" TRAIN

9. **Jumbles:** OBESE DRYLY FROLIC IODINE
   Answer: What the blushing bride was turning, whichever way one looked—REDDER

10. **Jumbles:** VALVE MADAM WHENCE FLORID
    Answer: Everybody was in debt but it's permitted—"ALL-OWED"

11. **Jumbles:** DERBY GLORY HANDLE FACING
    Answer: Sounds like a fisherman's dance—A REEL

12. **Jumbles:** MAGIC VAGUE CRAFTY NAUSEA
    Answer: What a person who loses his head would have difficulty doing—SAVING FACE

13. **Jumbles:** CYNIC HAVEN CORPSE BUMPER
    Answer: Ways that go straight to the heart—VEINS

14. **Jumbles:** BROOD MOLDY COMPEL NOVICE
    Answer: The snob was insulted when the doctor told him he was merely suffering from this—A "COMMON" COLD

15. **Jumbles:** MOUNT EJECT LATEST THROAT
    Answer: Might be three that could put you out—"ETHER"

16. **Jumbles:** IDIOT CHEEK POETRY DRIVEL
    Answer: How he protested when they put him in the cooler—HOTLY

17. **Jumbles:** MADLY PIKER OPPOSE BICEPS
    Answer: It might be "ill-gotten"—SICK PAY

18. **Jumbles:** RIVET VIPER INVITE LAUNCH
    Answer: The warden guaranteed the entertainers that the audience would be this—A "CAPTIVE" ONE

19. **Jumbles:** MERCY PHONY INBORN DEPICT
    Answer: How the executioner would have preferred getting to work—BY CHOPPER

20. **Jumbles:** POACH GROOM ORIGIN RADIUM
    Answer: What some comedians make—DOUGH OUT OF CORN

21. **Jumbles:** PIECE WEARY HECKLE CASKET
    Answer: What they called that eccentric cabdriver—A WACKY HACKIE

22. **Jumbles:** WHEAT ACRID MEMORY LAWFUL
    Answer: What those Eskimos loved to do at dinnertime—CHEW THE FAT

23. **Jumbles:** BUSHY TOKEN MAKEUP ACHING
    Answer: What it was for him when they repossessed the TV—A "SET BACK"

24. **Jumbles:** ABIDE FUSSY CENSUS GLOBAL
    Answer: What the boss was "breaking into"—"SOBS"

25. **Jumbles:** BUMPY FAULT CHISEL LOCALE
    Answer: How the waitress acted when she spilled the gravy—SAUCY

26. **Jumbles:** HONOR DUCAL COUSIN BALLAD
    Answer: When he became top banana he lost touch with this—THE OLD BUNCH

27. **Jumbles:** RANCH PORGY DENTAL JACKET
    Answer: What some not-so-young actors find it difficult to do—ACT THEIR AGE

28. **Jumbles:** TULLE QUASH GUIDED PUDDLE
    Answer: What happened after he bought a new pair of suspenders?—HE WAS HELD UP

29. **Jumbles:** MANGE WHOSE INDUCT EXODUS
    Answer: For not shoveling the sidewalk there—SNOW EXCUSE

30. **Jumbles:** PLAIT HENCE NOTIFY MAINLY
    Answer: What they called the guy who was nuts about fishing—A "FINN-ATIC"

31. **Jumbles:** FEINT AGING GARBLE TANGLE
    Answer: In a politician, the gift of gab is often connected with this—THE GIFT OF GRAB

32. **Jumbles:** RAJAH MURKY CATCHY HAIRDO
    Answer: In those years straw hats had this—THEIR "HAY" DAY

33. **Jumbles:** FORGO SIEGE ALWAYS INVOKE
    Answer: When they film a wintry scene in Hollywood, the prop man has to come up with plenty of these—SNOW FAKES

34. **Jumbles:** QUEER DOGMA BESIDE OUTLET
    Answer: People with tireless energy soon become this—TIRESOME

35. **Jumbles:** YOKEL WAGON BAFFLE GRIMLY
    Answer: What that golf nut had in his eyes—A "FAIR-WAY" LOOK

36. **Jumbles:** JOINT VALVE MUSKET HARBOR
    Answer: "I've finally bought you a watch for your birthday, dear"—"IT'S ABOUT TIME"

37. **Jumbles:** JUROR SORRY WIZARD PUMICE
    Answer: What they had to open in order to enter the haunted house—THE "SCREAM" DOOR

38. **Jumbles:** BRIAR KNAVE ACCESS TROUGH
    Answer: What it was for the peeping tom when he was caught looking through an open window—CURTAINS

39. **Jumbles:** EVOKE BYLAW KETTLE SICKEN
    Answer: Might be useful if you want to learn about the "shocking" secrets in that closet—A "SKELETON" KEY

40. **Jumbles:** NOOSE COWER WOBBLE CASKET
    Answer: What a name dropper is apt to do—BLOW HIS "KNOWS"

41. **Jumbles:** EXTOL VILLA TWINGE LETHAL
    Answer: What it sometimes takes to land a spouse—A LITTLE "WILE"

42. **Jumbles:** ELUDE JETTY FUSION BUSILY
    Answer: What a pillow salesman has to be a master of—THE SOFT SELL

43. **Jumbles:** BLANK AUDIT FUMBLE MODEST
    Answer: What the inventor of the first automatic packaging machine made—A BUNDLE

44. **Jumbles:** WRATH ABASH BUZZER PALACE
    Answer: What those old-time Russians fought—"CZAR" WARS

45. **Jumbles:** LIMIT BATON PUSHER TOTTER
    Answer: What the sugar tycoon got as he was trying to propose marriage—A LUMP IN HIS THROAT

46. **Jumbles:** BEGOT FORAY HAPPEN PARISH
    Answer: The only thing that children wear out faster than shoes—PARENTS

184

47. **Jumbles:** AMUSE FORCE WIDEST PRISON
Answer: What a bureaucrat is—A RED TAPE WORM

48. **Jumbles:** CURIO FAMED MANAGE PAROLE
Answer: Something a lot of women are taken in by—A GIRDLE

49. **Jumbles:** AGENT HOUSE FONDLY TOFFEE
Answer: How the traffic cop's girlfriend caught him—FLAT-FOOTED

50. **Jumbles:** JADED TANGY BRONCO INVADE
Answer: The media thought they'd better give the event plenty of this—"COVERAGE"

51. **Jumbles:** TRIPE FISHY SINFUL INVITE
Answer: How they celebrated the new year at that old-time saloon—WITH "FIST-IVITIES"

52. **Jumbles:** KINKY YIELD MISFIT PICKET
Answer: What part of a fish is like the end of a movie?—THE "FIN IS"

53. **Jumbles:** QUEST DUMPY INFECT FROTHY
Answer: What the karate champ turned restaurant owner specialized in—CHOPS

54. **Jumbles:** ORBIT WIPED LAWYER CLOVER
Answer: What the amazed spectators at the big game were—"BOWLED" OVER

55. **Jumbles:** CEASE FANCY EXHALE MUFFIN
Answer: After she asked him to start working on the garden, the first thing he dug up was this—AN EXCUSE

56. **Jumbles:** HUMID SNACK LADING ALWAYS
Answer: He listened to this while he practiced—SWING MUSIC

57. **Jumbles:** FRAME TAWNY PRIMED LATEST
Answer: The result of spending a fortune on workouts—LEAN TIMES

58. **Jumbles:** DITTY REARM AROUSE CORNER
Answer: What plumbing work can do to the family budget—CAUSE A DRAIN

59. **Jumbles:** TOOTH LEGAL MUFFIN OMELET
Answer: What the crowd experienced at the comedy club—A "LIGHT" MOMENT

60. **Jumbles:** CLOVE ABASH CUPFUL GYPSUM
Answer: Found at the shore—GULLS AND BUOYS

61. **Jumbles:** BUMPY AISLE MAINLY NESTLE
Answer: Hard to find on a shady person-A SUNNY SMILE

62. **Jumbles:** DOUGH PARTY TWINGE NORMAL
Answer: The kind of advice you get from an old farmer—DOWN TO EARTH

63. **Jumbles:** INKED SUEDE CHISEL UNFOLD
Answer: What she felt like when her husband concentrated on his music—SECOND FIDDLE

64. **Jumbles:** AMUSE CREEK REFUGE FASTEN
Answer: Tough for a garbage man to do—REFUSE REFUSE

65. **Jumbles:** ABOVE LATHE BEHEAD CHALET
Answer: Why the cop was in the jazz club—HE HAD THE BEAT

66. **Jumbles:** AGATE BILGE MULISH LANCER
Answer: What they heard around the fireplace on a cold night—A CHILLING TALE

67. **Jumbles:** GUMBO BRAVE SUCKLE VERMIN
Answer: A new computer inevitably has one of these—A CURSER

68. **Jumbles:** DAILY CAKED VACANT SLEIGH
Answer: Something actors look forward to—A CASTING CALL

69. **Jumbles:** DECAY ABBOT BROKEN PURITY
Answer: What the salesman did when they charged their purchases—TOOK THE "CREDIT"

70. **Jumbles:** PIOUS BERTH POUNCE APIECE
Answer: What a pretty flower arrangement can be—A "SCENT-ERPIECE"

71. **Jumbles:** LEECH AUGUR SWERVE BAFFLE
Answer: How the model calculated her worth—AT FACE VALUE

72. **Jumbles:** FLORA SCOUT OUTWIT KERNEL
Answer: Why the paper hanger worked late—HE WAS ON A ROLL

73. **Jumbles:** KHAKI MOTIF JOCUND INTAKE
Answer: What he got from his karate class—A KICK OUT OF IT

74. **Jumbles:** POKER GROUP ORIOLE LICHEN
Answer: Hooking a two hundred pound fish can leave you like this—REELING

75. **Jumbles:** SHYLY LOOSE FABRIC AIRWAY
Answer: This helped his yacht sail smoothly—CASH "FLOW"

76. **Jumbles:** RODEO STUNG DAMPEN THRIVE
Answer: The server found the diner's order this—HARD TO DIGEST

77. **Jumbles:** ROBOT BEIGE SURTAX MUSLIN
Answer: Stuck in a snowdrift left him—STORMING

78. **Jumbles:** FENCE WAGER MOHAIR TALLOW
Answer: A good thing to do when encountering an iceberg—GO WITH THE FLOE

79. **Jumbles:** TYPED UNWED HARDLY TERROR
Answer: What the romantic setting led to—A "HOT" DATE

80. **Jumbles:** LOGIC TIGER SALOON GRASSY
Answer: Always a concern for a careful balloonist—SOARING COSTS

81. **Jumbles:** KNAVE PUTTY GUTTER MUSEUM
Answer: What a novice tailor wants to do—MEASURE UP

82. **Jumbles:** CREEL PEACE TARTAR BALLAD
Answer: A good way to grab dinner in a supermarket—A LA "CART"

83. **Jumbles:** LIGHT ALIVE HELIUM PILFER
Answer: What the plastic surgery did—GAVE HER A "LIFT"

84. **Jumbles:** BASIN VISOR ENCAMP RANCID
Answer: A quarterback makes this in every huddle—A SNAP DECISION

85. **Jumbles:** PERKY CHAOS EXOTIC PUDDLE
Answer: What the new photographer sought for his work—EXPOSURE

86. **Jumbles:** LOFTY WHOSE WIZARD JARGON
Answer: This helps when working on a home computer—"SOFT"-WARE

87. **Jumbles:** GIVEN OAKEN PITIED FESTAL
Answer: What a creative gardener likes to do—PLANT IDEAS

88. **Jumbles:** GRAIN FRIAR KISMET DELUXE
Answer: How he described the shapely girl at the ice rink—A "FIGURE" SKATER

89. **Jumbles:** TROTH SHOWY CLOUDY RANCOR
Answer: What the football team experienced after a bumpy flight—A TOUCH DOWN

90. **Jumbles:** LARVA THICK BARROW CONCUR
Answer: Employees on a cruise ship do this all the time—WORK ON A VACATION

91. **Jumbles:** ELITE SQUAB POETIC INTENT
Answer: What the irate customers gave the phone company—A LOT OF STATIC

92. **Jumbles:** SURLY DOGMA LIQUOR BYWORD
Answer: Something a wise guy usually lacks—WISDOM

93. **Jumbles:** DRONE HABIT MEADOW BANANA
Answer: What the outrageous rock group became—A BANNED BAND

94. **Jumbles:** CHOKE PLAIT SAILOR MAGNET
Answer: One too many drinks caused him to do this—SLEEP "TIGHT"

95. **Jumbles:** IRATE PECAN RAVAGE EXTANT
Answer: Watching the tattoo artist became this—PENETRATING

96. **Jumbles:** GAMUT CRUSH BEHALF ELICIT
Answer: What a haunted house becomes on Halloween—A FRIGHT SITE

97. **Jumbles:** FACET CASTE PREACH SOCIAL
Answer: This will make a lawyer successful—LOST OF "PRACTICE"

98. **Jumbles:** PRIME TWEET FAMOUS MARAUD
Answer: Easy to feel like this working in the Everglades—SWAMPED

99. **Jumbles:** ADMIT HAREM BUOYED ENOUGH
Answer: What the animal rights group did to the fox hunters—HOUNDED THEM

100. **Jumbles:** TWICE SHINY HOOKUP BEFOUL
Answer: When the roofer pitched in to help his neighbor, it was—ON THE HOUSE

101. **Jumbles:** HEFTY TYING HIDING ENGINE
Answer: What the competing hotel owners got involved in—INN FIGHTING

102. **Jumbles:** PIVOT LISLE SEETHE TAMPER
Answer: The best way to build a staircase with a do-it-yourself kit—STEP BY STEP

103. **Jumbles:** FANCY DAUNT ERMINE REDUCE
Answer: He got the job as a piano mover although he couldn't even do this—CARRY A TUNE

104. **Jumbles:** RIVET COLON PAYING SUBTLY
Answer: A hard working garbage man doesn't mind when his boss does this—PILES IT ON

105. **Jumbles:** PRIZE PAYEE SMOKER HAGGLE
Answer: What the tired passengers turned the coach car into—A SLEEPER

106. **Jumbles:** BURST EXTOL TRICKY BOUGHT
Answer: The lawyer didn't want to do this during the trial—COURT TROUBLE

107. **Jumbles:** QUOTA GUILD ASSURE ATOMIC
Answer: A chimney sweep wears this to work—A SOOT SUIT

108. **Jumbles:** MESSY JOUST BROKER INVOKE
Answer: What she considered the fortune teller—A SITE SEER

109. **Jumbles:** NERVY BATCH PODIUM CAMPUS
Answer: A good way to relax on the weekend—PAINT THE HOUSE

110. **Jumbles:** CHANT BANAL PURVEY CAMPER
Answer: What the animals enjoyed—THE HUMAN RACE

111. **Jumbles:** KNIFE SIXTY FAULTY GROUCH
Answer: Upholstering a chair can be this—"TACKS-ING" WORK

112. **Jumbles:** CHUTE CYNIC SCHEME JETSAM
Answer: What mom enjoyed while doing the linens—"SHEET" MUSIC

113. **Jumbles:** JERKY ANNOY EASILY KINGLY
Answer: Important to know before trying the new fad diet—THE SKINNY

114. **Jumbles:** COACH TRUTH PARITY OUTFIT
Answer: Steamy weather can turn into this on the news—A HOT TOPIC

115. **Jumbles:** DRAWL GROIN NUDISM SPONGE
Answer: The result of wearing casual clothes to a formal meeting—A DRESSING DOWN

116. **Jumbles:** PARCH CLEFT JOBBER POTENT
Answer: Building a dog house for Fido turned into this—A PET PROJECT

117. **Jumbles:** FELON JULEP BUTTON EFFACE
Answer: She doesn't drink coffee because it's—NOT HER CUP OF TEA

118. **Jumbles:** PYLON AUDIT OUTING FITFUL
Answer: What the muscle man considered his victory—UPLIFTING

119. **Jumbles:** BLIMP WHOOP MEMOIR MATURE
Answer: The absent-minded professor had plenty of this—ROOM AT THE TOP

120. **Jumbles:** FORAY SWOON NOTIFY JUNKET
Answer: This happened to his career when he became a pilot—IT TOOK OFF

121. **Jumbles:** JEWEL TRULY FAMISH BELIEF
Answer: What the cameraman captured on his photo of moonshiners—A "STILL" LIFE

122. **Jumbles:** ADAGE SORRY SHAKEN CURFEW
Answer: Why the locksmith's computer didn't work—HE USED THE WRONG KEY

123. **Jumbles:** SHAKY TASTY EMBARK JOCKEY
Answer: When it comes to contests her dessert does this-TAKES THE CAKE

124. **Jumbles:** RURAL LINGO VENDOR DAINTY
Answer: What the successful politician excelled at—RUNNING

125. **Jumbles:** WRATH PIETY NINETY DUGOUT
Answer: You are usually required to pay this in college—ATTENTION

126. **Jumbles:** DUSKY CATCH BUTANE DULCET
Answer: What the boss did when business got slow—CUT BACK

127. **Jumbles:** EXCEL OPERA BANGLE KINDLY
Answer: How the holiday gift-wrapper felt—BOXED IN

128. **Jumbles:** YACHT TRIPE EQUITY INFECT
Answer: This can be tough when the meat is tender—THE PRICE

129. **Jumbles:** TARRY UNCLE BECAME AROUND
Answer: What the grocer got when he lowered the price on detergent—CLEANED OUT

130. **Jumbles:** GOURD LAUGH YEARLY FLABBY
Answer: What Christmas is for many—A HOLLY DAY

131. **Jumbles:** BRINY SUAVE POLICY DECODE
Answer: What the crooked politician was involved in when he painted his office—A COVER UP

132. **Jumbles:** FAUNA BANDY BARREL HECKLE
Answer: Belt tightening calls for this—A BUCKLE

133. **Jumbles:** UTTER BOGUS SHREWD PYTHON
Answer: What the philosopher turned diver had before submerging—"DEEP" THOUGHTS

134. **Jumbles:** MERGE RAINY ADROIT LIMPID
Answer: This will avoid alimony—MATRIMONY

135. **Jumbles:** SNORT BULGY CALICO BEWARE
Answer: What she did when the wind broke her beach umbrella—A SLOW BURN

136. **Jumbles:** SWOOP ENACT AUTHOR LARYNX
Answer: A noon-time workout can turn unto this—A "POWER" LUNCH

137. **Jumbles:** CUBIC RUSTY FOSSIL TANKER
Answer: A good way to comply with a school dress code—SKIRT THE ISSUE

138. **Jumbles:** GRIEF AFIRE BUNION VERBAL
Answer: When the king tamed the wild horse he proved that he was—THE "REINING" RULER

139. **Jumbles:** ELEGY TOOTH CAVORT UNSAID
Answer: A person who makes little things count—A TEACHER

140. **Jumbles:** STEED IRATE GUNNER MARROW
Answer: What jaywalkers may be wearing tomorrow—WINGS

141. **Jumbles:** CAPON RAPID NUDISM TIMELY
Answer: What the egoist was suffering from—"I" STRAIN

142. **Jumbles:** SHAKY HOARD MOTIVE JESTER
Answer: What the cute little potato was warned against—MASHERS

143. **Jumbles:** MOSSY GROUP MORGUE EITHER
Answer: What boarding house gossip used to start with—"ROOMERS"

144. **Jumbles:** BASSO ARMOR TACKLE STUCCO
Answer: What the twelve bottles of moonshine eventually became—A COURT CASE

145. **Jumbles:** FUDGE VISTA UNCLAD ENTICE
Answer: Rather big for ballet these days—AUDIENCES

146. **Jumbles:** MOUNT FILMY INFIRM GALAXY
Answer: What horsemeat is to a dog—"FILLY" MIGNON

147. **Jumbles:** MEALY GUESS PURIFY ENTAIL
Answer: We close our eyes to this—SLEEP

148. **Jumbles:** BLIMP HOBBY NIMBLE DRAGON
Answer: Where the overzealous cow gave her milk—BEYOND THE "PAIL"

149. **Jumbles:** HABIT MADAM GUITAR FORMAL
Answer: Someone who raids the refrigerator for a midnight snack—A "HAM-BURGLAR"

150. **Jumbles:** LINGO UNWED HERMIT CRAYON
Answer: It's usual to have this before dinner—LUNCH

151. **Jumbles:** WHEEL EMBER BIKINI LARYNX
Answer: What the traveling correspondent's wife didn't like—HIS "BYE LINE"

152. **Jumbles:** DRAFT EMPTY INVERT REFUGE
Answer: You can always grow this in your garden if you work hard enough—TIRED

153. **Jumbles:** IMBUE CHOKE TANGLE DOUBLY
Answer: Something besides the tide which the moon affects—THE UNTIED

154. **Jumbles:** COWER JULEP TRIBAL ANEMIA
Answer: What you might call this barber's establishment—A CLIP JOINT

155. **Jumbles:** RODEO FAVOR THIRTY BRIDLE
Answer: What she called her sourpuss husband—HER BITTER HALF

156. **Jumbles:** PROVE FETID NIBBLE ORIGIN
Answer: The boxer's smooth line finally got him this—ROPED IN

157. **Jumbles:** CARGO KNIFE PEPTIC KITTEN
Answer: A man whose work requires him to grasp things quickly—A PICKPOCKET

158. **Jumbles:** GROOM FOAMY NUANCE SINGLE
Answer: What her earnings often don't keep up with—HER YEARNINGS

159. **Jumbles:** ALIVE OFTEN DREDGE CAMPUS
Answer: What the sailor became when he married a widow—A SECOND MATE

160. **Jumbles:** CLOUT ALBUM FAÇADE HOMAGE
Answer: What it takes to get these two all fired up—A MATCH

161. **Jumbles:** FORCED NEGATE BESIDE CALLOW OBJECT FLAGON
Answer: He got fired from his job for lying—TOO LONG IN BED

162. **Jumbles:** AROUND TRAGIC ASYLUM BOTHER JARGON VOYAGE
Answer: His mother-in-law's shortcoming was this—HER "LONG STAYING"

163. **Jumbles:** EMPLOY SCENIC BANANA GUTTER CLEAVE DEMISE
Answer: The first duty of the missionary was to convert the cannibals to this—VEGETARIANISM

164. **Jumbles:** CLUMSY TRIBAL ACCENT BOLERO SURELY QUARTZ
Answer: The kind of people you might meet at the information bureau—"QUESTIONABLE" ONES

165. **Jumbles:** JERSEY CUPFUL PALLID VENDOR ABLAZE BEMOAN
Answer: What that love letter was calculated to do—SPEED UP THE "MALE"

166. **Jumbles:** GAMBLE INDUCT ALPACA LOTION DEFACE NICELY
Answer: Nothing gets a person all up in the air quicker than this—AN INFLATED EGO

167. **Jumbles:** GLOOMY CLOVER VERMIN OBLIGE AERATE LAWYER
Answer: That ancient statue phone his insurance broker because he needed this—MORE COVERAGE

168. **Jumbles:** PRAYER SWERVE MAINLY CIPHER FLIMSY EXOTIC
Answer: Home cooking is what a man misses when this happens—HIS WIFE ISN'T

169. **Jumbles:** DECEIT TUXEDO SINGLE BEETLE LIQUID BEFALL
Answer: Important for her business lunch—A "SUIT-ABLE" OUTFIT

170. **Jumbles:** NIMBLE NAUGHT BASKET SECOND NEARLY BISECT
Answer: The art of magic is—A TRICKY BUSINESS

171. **Jumbles:** MUFFLE BUSHEL BAKING AUTUMN MARLIN RADIAL
Answer: Some dermatologists often do this—GET UNDER YOUR SKIN

172. **Jumbles:** CUDDLE LEGUME ENMITY GRATIS PREFIX AUBURN
Answer: What the financiers invested in at the racetrack—A PARI-MUTUEL FUND

173. **Jumbles:** ORIOLE EXTANT CLOUDY MARMOT CAMPUS UNLESS
Answer: What he considered the expensive sports car—PRECIOUS METAL

174. **Jumbles:** TIMING NEEDLE INSIST UNWISE HOMING MUSEUM
Answer: Why the statesmen met at a mountain resort—FOR A SUMMIT MEETING

175. **Jumbles:** POUNCE SOCIAL JUSTLY BARIUM SUPERB MAGNET
Answer: Enjoyed by the movie star on her fishing trip—A SUPPORTING CAST

176. **Jumbles:** WEEVIL SWERVE TURTLE TALKER CYMBAL DISARM
Answer: The golfer turned into this when his tee shot went astray—A RECKLESS DRIVER

177. **Jumbles:** BRANDY POROUS CELERY GRIMLY THRESH STYMIE
Answer: Sculpting an X-rated statue made him this—A DIRTY CHISELER

178. **Jumbles:** ATTAIN ORIGIN DISMAL POETRY TURNIP ENTITY
Answer: What the model wanted to end up doing—SITTING PRETTY

179. **Jumbles:** BICKER GARLIC FROLIC WIDEST HANDED JUGGLE
Answer: Often obtained from a job counselor—A "HIRE" EDUCATION

180. **Jumbles:** BANNER BODILY WISELY DEMURE FINERY CROUCH
Answer: What he did when she bought him gaudy suspenders—"BRACED" HIMSELF

Need More Jumbles®?

Order any of these books through your bookseller or call Triumph Books toll-free at 800-335-5323.

Jumble® Books

More than 175 puzzles each!

Animal Jumble®
$9.95 • ISBN 1-57243-197-0

Jumble® at Work
$9.95 • ISBN 1-57243-147-4

Jumble® Fever
$9.95 • ISBN 1-57243-593-3

Jumble® Fiesta
$9.95 • ISBN 1-57243-626-3

Jumble® Fun
$9.95 • ISBN 1-57243-379-5

Jumble® Grab Bag
$9.95 • ISBN 1-57243-273-X

Jumble® Jamboree
$9.95 • ISBN 1-57243-696-4

Jumble® Jubilee
$9.95 • ISBN 1-57243-231-4

Jumble® Junction
$9.95 • ISBN 1-57243-380-9

Jumble® Madness
$9.95 • ISBN 1-892049-24-4

Jumble® Mania
$9.95 • ISBN 1-57243-697-2

Jumble® See & Search
$9.95 • ISBN 1-57243-549-6

Jumble® Surprise
$9.95 • ISBN 1-57243-320-5

Romance Jumble®
$9.95 • ISBN 1-57243-146-6

Sports Jumble®
$9.95 • ISBN 1-57243-113-X

Summer Fun Jumble®
$9.95 • ISBN 1-57243-114-8

Travel Jumble®
$9.95 • ISBN 1-57243-198-9

TV Jumble®
$9.95 • ISBN 1-57243-461-9

Oversize Jumble® Books

Colossal Jumble®
$19.95 • ISBN 1-57243-490-2

Generous Jumble®
$19.95 • ISBN 1-57243-385-X

Giant Jumble®
$19.95 • ISBN 1-57243-349-3

Gigantic Jumble®
$19.95 • ISBN 1-57243-426-0

Jumbo Jumble®
$19.95 • ISBN 1-57243-314-0

More than 500 puzzles each!

Jumble® Crosswords™

More than 175 puzzles each!

Jumble® Crosswords™
$9.95 • ISBN 1-57243-347-7

More Jumble® Crosswords™
$9.95 • ISBN 1-57243-386-8

Jumble® Crosswords™ Adventure
$9.95 • ISBN 1-57243-462-7

Jumble® Crosswords™ Challenge
$9.95 • ISBN 1-57243-423-6

Jumble® Crosswords™ Jackpot
$9.95 • ISBN 1-57243-615-8

Jumble® BrainBusters™

Jumble® BrainBusters™
$9.95 • ISBN: 1-892049-28-7

Jumble® BrainBusters™ II
$9.95 • ISBN: 1-57243-424-4

Jumble® BrainBusters™ III
$9.95 • ISBN: 1-57243-463-5

Jumble® BrainBusters™ IV
$9.95 • ISBN: 1-57243-489-9

Jumble® BrainBusters™ 5
$9.95 • ISBN: 1-57243-548-8

Hollywood Jumble® BrainBusters™
$9.95 • ISBN: 1-57243-594-1

Jumble® BrainBusters™ Bonanza
$9.95 • ISBN: 1-57243-616-6

Boggle™ BrainBusters™
$9.95 • ISBN: 1-57243-592-5

Jumble® BrainBusters™ Junior
$9.95 • ISBN: 1-892049-29-5

Jumble® BrainBusters™ Junior II
$9.95 • ISBN: 1-57243-425-2

More than 175 puzzles each!